PRAISE FOR *THE RIPPLE EFFECT*

"In *The Ripple Effect*, Steve Harper taps into one of the most powerful truths of successful business: doing the little things to keep customers happy and engaged will have a tremendous impact on your company's long-term growth and profitability. *The Ripple Effect* is a must-read for anyone who wants to attract and keep customers for life."

— **Bill Stinnett**
   Author of the best-selling *Think Like Your Customer*

"If people would only read, and apply, the lessons in *The Ripple Effect*, it would not only be a better world to live in, we would all be more successful."

— **Terry A. Britton**
   Co-author of *Priceless: Turning Ordinary Products into Extraordinary Experiences*

"Steve has an amazing way of demonstrating the ebb and flow of life experiences. His stories touch all aspects of how karma and action go hand in hand. *The Ripple Effect* will profoundly influence the way you think and behave."

— **Kelsey August**
   CEO, Lone Star Direct (an INC. 500 company)
   Author of *Mad at Martha*

"Steve Harper is the 'Relationship Guru!' In his new book, Steve reminds us of the importance of relationships in our lives. He explains how *everyone* can build powerful relationships, especially when we understand our own and others' core energy."

— **Bijoy Goswami**
   Author of *The Human Fabric: Unleashing the Power of Core Energy in Everyone*

The
RIPPLE
EFFECT

Stephanie —

Thanks for Rippling!

Ripple On!!!

Steve Harper

The

RIPPLE
EFFECT

Maximizing the Power of Relationships
for Your Life and Business

Steve Harper

SWOT
publishing

ISBN: 0-9768665-0-1

Library of Congress Control Number: 2005903390

Printed in the United States of America

Layout: Think Write Communications
www.think-write.net

Cover design: XCELARTS
www.xcelarts.com

SWOT Publishing
300 S. Kettleman Lane
Austin, TX 78717

SWOT
publishing

www.therippleeffectbook.com

"The people that influence us become the brush strokes of the masterpiece we paint called our life."

This is my first book and it truly has been a labor of love. I know that none of it would have been possible without the support, love and encouragement of my wife, Kathy. Through her I have been able to learn how to be myself and be comfortable in my own skin. Thank you, Kathy, for being in my life and giving what you have so that I can continue to pursue my dreams. I love you!

I also dedicate this book to my two sons, Zachary and Joshua. Guys, I love you both so very much and want this world to be a wonderful, amazing place for you to grow up in. I know that because of you more positive ripples come my way every single day.

To Dad, who is, without question, one of my all-time heroes. I strive to be the man that you are and have shown me to be. I can only hope to equal the amazing ripples you started for so many. Thank you for all the lessons you have given me. Your courage, faith and dedication are an inspiration to me.

To Mom; although, because of your disease, you will likely never read the words in this book, it is because of you and your talents that I have found the courage to write it. I love you and miss our "chats" more than you will ever know.

Finally, to someone who had such an important impact in my life, Jay Stephenson. You will always be "Mr. J" to me, and I count my lucky stars that you saw something in me way back in high school and never refused to give up on me. You taught me the possibilities of business and that anything can be mine if I want it badly enough. Well, Jay, this book has come to fruition because of you and all that you have done to influence my life. Thank you for everything!

TABLE OF CONTENTS

ACKNOWLEDGMENTS

There are so many people who have positively influenced me that it would be impossible to list them all here. Without you and the ripples you created in my life, this book would not have been possible. I hope you all know, even without me saying it, how much I appreciate and cherish having you in my life, and how grateful I am for what you have done for me both personally and professionally.

Marc Schwarz, you and I began this journey not really knowing where it might lead us. After some trial and error and a lot of brainstorming, it has developed into a piece of work of which I think we can both be extremely proud. You have taken my sometimes clumsy sentences and created music out of my thoughts, words and concepts. You have been a real godsend on this project, and I am so truly grateful for all that you have done. I'm even more grateful for the friendship and "dance" we've developed with one another. I look so forward to all of our future projects — and there is without a doubt so much more to do and to say. Thank you, my friend.

Wayne Henderson, my friend, my mentor — without you, my early years in business would have been horrible at best. You took me under your wing and treated me as an equal in so many ways and, despite some of my ego-driven ideas and decisions, never gave up on me. In your role as my unofficial therapist, you encouraged me to spread my wings when it was time, and you knew just when to yank me back (likely before my wings took me through that glass window)!

Kelsey, you have been a long-standing friend, business associate, supporter and an unbelievable mentor. I cherish what we have together and the opportunities we are only beginning to discover by working together. There really is a "power in two" and the combination we form is dangerous! Thank you so much for all that you have given to me. There will never be enough opportunity to repay you for all that you have done — but you know I'll do my best to try!

Maura, your friendship and support is simply amazing. Through our interactions, we have truly shown the power of what a relationship can do. I appreciate your tremendous input and dedication to watching this process come to light.

Bijoy, we were meant to meet and work together — I am sure of it. I count my lucky stars that you are in my life and that you continue to challenge and inspire me every day. Our two unique perspectives on this world create such amazing opportunities for discussion, debate and action. I'm certain that the ripples we create together will be simply amazing. I can't wait to see what amazing things lie ahead of us.

Lack of space keeps me from acknowledging more of the people I've worked with in the past. But you know who you are, and hopefully you know how much each of you means to me. Loyalty and hard work do go hand in hand. I'll never forget what each of you has done and continues to do for me. From the bottom of my heart, THANK YOU!

A LIFE WELL LIVED

How you will you be remembered?

Many, if not most, people tend avoid thinking about death and dying forced to by circumstances beyond their control. That's pretty natural, I guess, and probably not unhealthy.

But although I don't sit around daydreaming about my own eventual demise, I do have a picture in mind of how I'd like it to be: me peacefully, quietly drifting off, surrounded by my family and friends and even some cherished possessions, my spirit soaring to a new time and place as my last breath leaves my body.

Mind you, I'm hoping that won't happen for a long, long time. But I believe that whatever you're doing, no matter what it is, you must have an end firmly in mind even before you begin. Whether you're making a quick run to the store for a couple of items or setting off on a long trip, it's wise to know what your goals are up front. If you don't, chances are you're going to miss something critical along the way.

That same philosophy applies to our careers and our lives. Whether you're angling for a promotion or simply want to experience all the joy and wonder that life has to offer, you had best start with the end in mind. And part of that is thinking about how you want to be remembered. Is where you are today where you want to be tomorrow?

Just for a few minutes, forget that fear of dying and look at your life from the outside. If your time were up tomorrow, what kind of legacy would you leave behind? Besides your friends, who would miss you? Apart from your family, who would mourn for you? And who, ultimately, would have benefited from knowing you? How many lives would your life have touched?

Would anyone pay attention to your passing, or would it go unnoticed by a world more concerned about where it's going to eat dinner tonight or what's on TV? Would anyone care about your accomplishments, or would they just thumb over your obituary to get to the business section or sports page? Five years after your passing, would your memory — your presence — still live on?

Hard questions to answer and, sometimes, hard answers to face. Fortunately, there's still time to change your life for the better. If you're not where you want to be, it's not too late — yet. But personal growth doesn't come easily or painlessly.

Several years ago I asked myself those same questions, and I didn't like the answers I was forced to give. So I consciously made some changes. I was fortunate to have some great people in my life who helped and encouraged me along the way. It's been those connections that have made my success, my satisfaction and this book possible.

If you're not where you want to be, it's not too late — yet.

Thanks to those changes, my endgame plays out a little differently now. Take my funeral, for instance. In my imagination, I visualize the crowd filling the church to capacity. Rather than quiet and somber, they are actually almost joyful. It'll feel like a reunion as old friends and acquaintances gather, not to mourn my passing, but to celebrate the life I lived and the legacy I leave them all. There will be smiles and hugs and handshakes — and no tears! And even if I won't be there to physically take part, I know my spirit will be watching and smiling as I feel all the love and affection poured out on me and my memory.

I know this is more fantasy than reality. The fact is, too many funerals I've attended seemed consciously or unconsciously designed to be sad, not joyful. You wear dark clothes, you speak in hushed tones and you mumble comforting words. I've always assumed that somewhere on the prayer card they hand you as you walk into the church is, in microscopic type, something that says, "You have now entered the church. Please find a seat and commence with being sad. Tears are optional but encouraged. Whatever you do, you should absolutely never, under any circumstances, smile. Please remember to do your part in making this service a sad and somber occasion."

I always thought that that was a little misguided. Sure, someone you cared about isn't around any more to talk with you or hug you or spend time with you. That finality is certainly sad.

But the flip side of the coin is that a funeral is also an opportunity to celebrate a life well lived. Even though our physical bodies break down, I believe our spirit and memory live on in the lives we've touched. In my imaginary funeral, the friends and family present are living treasure chests, filled with good memories of our time together. As long as they continue to cherish those memories, I'll never be truly gone. I'll continue to impact the lives of the people I cared about long after my body has turned to dust. That's something I find both reassuring and powerful.

I don't dwell on my death, and I'm not encouraging you to do so either. But I believe that it is relevant to think about the kind

> **The connections we form with the people around us, whether at home, in the office or on the playground, define the pattern of our lives.**

of lasting impression you'll leave on this world. How will you be remembered? And by whom?

Our lives are a smorgasbord of experiences and memories. And what links them all together is people: the people who have touched us and the people we've touched in return. The connections we form with the people around us, whether at home, in the office or on the playground, define the pattern of our lives. It's the *relationships* in our lives — with God, with ourselves, with our family and friends, with our co-workers, even with casual acquaintances — that matter most. Period.

And that's what I want at my funeral: people I care about saying thanks one more time, not just by saying goodbye, but by coming together to celebrate the bonds we shared. Forget politeness or proper etiquette! I want real feeling — good feeling — instead of a bunch of hollow, hackneyed accolades.

I hope that that's what you want to do as well: to leave something of real value behind and to be remembered for the good you did and the lives you impacted. For me, that realization became a driving force for positive personal change.

I also realized that it's not just the major decisions in your life that impact others. Virtually everything you do has some effect on someone, somewhere. It's like throwing a stone into a pond and watching the ripples spread outward until they touch the shore. And even the smallest pebble produces ripples. They may be imperceptible, but they're there. Once I really embraced that image as a symbol of how my life intersected with and influenced others, I began to see some amazing things happen both in my life and in the lives of others.

This ripple effect isn't limited to one part of your life. It applies equally well to the office, the home, church, casual social settings, even your kids' Little League games. It's a subtle but powerful force that affects our entire existence.

"The good man makes others good."

— *Greek proverb*

And it doesn't have to be random. I realized that we can consciously harness the ripple effect to create positive changes in the world, one person at a time, one thoughtful action at a time.

In taking the time to help others, I found that my own life became happier, more satisfying and more meaningful. My businesses prospered, new opportunities opened up and long-held anxieties receded. New or newly-deepened relationships suddenly offered a world of possibilities.

That can happen for you, too. There are unbelievable opportunities in everyone you know, everyone you love — and in everyone you just happen to meet today at Starbucks. If you never take the time to recognize, much less act on, those relationship opportunities, well, that really is something to mourn.

In the pages that follow, you'll find the seeds for creating a new, more productive, more satisfying life for yourself. If you plant those seeds and nurture them, you'll see your personal and professional success grow. You'll enjoy your days more, enjoy your work more, enjoy your family more. Your confidence, commitment and motivation will all increase.

And, over time, your relationships will blossom into something truly beautiful, something that will never fade, never die and will never leave you without color in your life. Isn't that worth the time?

PART 1

Developing a
Relationship Mindset

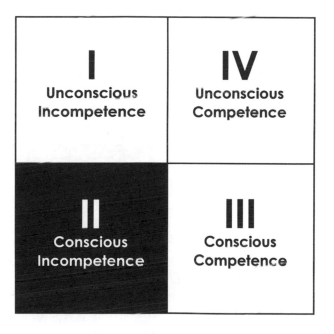

I Unconscious Incompetence	**IV** Unconscious Competence
II Conscious Incompetence	**III** Conscious Competence

We learn in four stages:

I Unconscious incompetence
This is a state of blissful ignorance. Although we are not knowledgeable or skillful, our confidence exceeds our ability. Put simply, we don't know that we don't know.

II Conscious incompetence
We discover a skill we wish to learn and our confidence plummets as we realize our ignorance and limitations: we know that we don't know. Learning requires practice, which often results in failure and frustration. Without this step, painful as it usually is, we cannot acquire new skills.

III Conscious competence
In this stage, we acquire the skill. We have to focus on the task to accomplish it, however; it doesn't yet come naturally. Our confidence increases with our ability. We know that we know how to do something.

IV Unconscious competence
Lastly, we blend skills together and they become habits — we can then do them well while our mind is on other things. The skill has become a natural part of ourselves, and our confidence and ability peaks. We no longer have to concentrate on processes or formulas.

These four stages apply equally to learning to drive a car or play the piano or maximizing the power of relationships. Learning takes time and involves practice, which often means mistakes and frustrations. Understanding and utilizing the ripple effect is no different. But the ultimate payoff is well worth the short-term aggravation.

This book is divided into three distinct sections. In Part 1, the goal is to help you move from unconscious incompetence to conscious incompetence. Chances are you've ignored too many relationship opportunities in your life and business

— time to see what you're missing. In Part 2, you'll begin to develop some relationship-building skills as you move from conscious incompetence to conscious competence. And finally, with the habits and tools in Part 3, you'll be on your way to moving from conscious competence to the final and highest stage of learning: unconscious competence.

It all starts with your decision to turn the page . . .

On a cold November evening in 1965, a small metal cup inside a rectangular box at a power station in Niagara Falls began to slowly revolve. A tiny metal arm set in the center of the cup also began rotating, coming closer and closer to a metal contact. Only a handful of people even knew where and what the cup was.

The cup was part of a backup electric power relay, set to trip if power levels exceeded a certain level. That level had been set two years previously, and although the system could now handle a much increased load, no one remembered to adjust the relay. So when power flowing to Toronto momentarily flickered above 375 megawatts, magnets inside the rectangular box reacted, and the cup began its slow but inevitable rotation.

When the metal arm struck the contact, the Toronto-bound power line was taken out of service, and the power rerouted to four other northbound power lines. That overloaded them, and their breakers tripped. Less than three seconds later, the power flowing north reversed direction into south- and eastbound lines heading into New York City and down the East Coast. Seriously overloaded, the entire system shut itself down.

Only 12 minutes had passed since the metal cup began its fateful rotation. The sequence of events it set in motion caused life to grind to a standstill in one of the richest and most heavily populated areas of the Western world. Over 30 million people were affected by the blackout, some for up to 13 hours. Some even died. And, as author James Burke wrote, "For all of them, life would never quite be the same again."

All because of a little metal cup inside a rectangular box.

1

UNEXPECTED TREASURES
*Personal and professional benefits
of relationship building*

The most powerful, the most successful, the most satisfying accomplishments in both your life and your business result from the relationships you form with the people in your world.

I know that's a pretty sweeping statement. But if this book is going to help you create the life and career you want, you've got to come to believe that. So just take a minute to really digest it: *The most powerful, the most successful, the most satisfying accomplishments in both your life and your business result from the relationships you form with the people in your world.*

Some of the results are direct and obvious, but a surprising number of them aren't. Don't think, though, that that subtlety makes them any less powerful. How many of us happened to find the right job thanks in part to some "friend of a friend?" How many of us met our spouses through a mutual acquaintance? How many opportunities have come our way because of who, not necessarily what, we know?

Virtually every people-oriented action we take produces a ripple effect, setting into motion a chain of events that can profoundly affect both our lives and others.

The Science of Ripples

Do you remember the first time you tossed a stone into a pond? Maybe it was a family camping trip, or during a weekend at the lake, or on a neighborhood street after a heavy rain. If you were like me, you probably watched in amazement as the ripples spread outward in ever expanding circles, until the whole surface of the water was set into motion. Visually, there's just something innately beautiful, fascinating and satisfying about seeing even a little pebble so dramatically influence its environment. But what's really happening here?

When the pebble hits the surface of the water, it transfers its kinetic energy (the result of the size of the pebble and the speed it was traveling) into the surrounding water molecules. That energy causes the molecules to move up and then back down at a fixed rate, which produces a wave. That energy is then transferred along intra-molecular bonds to other water molecules, which behave the same way. The water molecules are not permanently displaced from their original position — what we're really seeing is the movement of the energy itself.

Ripples radiate outward from the point of origin in a series of circles. The wider the circles become, the more dispersed the energy becomes and the less evident the ripples are. But that energy wave continues to spread long after we can no longer see its effects. It will spread, in fact, until it hits the shore, at which point the energy is reflected back and the ripples head back towards the source.

Physical ripples are about energy and movement, just like the relationship ripples we'll be talking about in this book. It's sometimes harder to see those relationship ripples in action, but that doesn't mean they're not working results every bit as dramatic as what happens when a stone hits the surface of a pond. The relationship energy set in motion by your actions is a powerful, provocative force.

Using the Ripple Effect

We often talk about ripple effects in politics, economics, religion and pop culture. Chances are that you've even experienced ripple effects on a more personal scale. Ever told a lie that seemed to take on a life of its own? You started a ripple effect. Ever played matchmaker for two friends who eventually married? You started a ripple effect. Ever referred business to a company you trust? You started a ripple effect.

In my own life, I can spot the ripple effects that allowed me to meet and marry my wife, start a couple of successful companies, create several mutually-beneficial business alliances, and forge a number of lasting friendships. I think you'll find the same is true in your life. Odds are that every major milestone was the result of an ever-expanding ripple effect.

> **The connections we form with the people around us, whether at home, in the office or on the playground, define the pattern of our lives.**

Because the ripple imagery is so familiar, we tend to underestimate its unique transformative power. But I can assure you that if you're prepared to understand it, embrace it and consciously use it in every facet of your life, it can have dramatic effects for you personally, for your business and for the people you care about. I've experienced it in my life and my career, and so can you. And it can all start with a small action — maybe even something as simple as picking up this book.

Ripple Rules

Just like in nature, our relationship ripples behave according to a specified set of rules. I've seen them work in my life and in the lives of those around me, and I think that if you just look closely enough, you'll see them in your life as well.

1. *Ripples can be caused by even the smallest pebbles.* It's not just your major decisions that impact others. Sometimes, just taking the time to talk to someone at Starbucks can have a big influence — whether or not you realize it.

Let me give you an example from my own life. Several years ago I was out in San Diego for a conference. During some downtime one morning, I was sitting on a group of rocks overlooking the beach, admiring the view and thinking about my business, when an elderly gentleman sat down on the rock next to me. I was a bit annoyed at having my solitude interrupted like that, and even more annoyed when he asked, "Where are you from?"

My mother raised me right, so I answered him politely, but I immediately turned my gaze back at the ocean, hoping he'd get the hint and leave me alone. Instead, he said, "The ocean's a powerful draw, isn't it? I love coming up here every morning and watching the day develop. It seems that no matter what your problems are, the ocean puts it all in perspective. The timing, the crashing of the waves, the rhythm of it all — it's God's instrument, the heart beat of life."

I stared at the man, amazed at his words. My annoyance, my impatience, my prejudice all seemed to wash away with the sound of the waves. He asked me a number of very direct and very personal questions, but he did it with such genuine and sincere interest that I didn't mind sharing the answers. For the next two and half hours I sat on that rock, listening, answering . . . and learning. It was one of the most profound — if least expected — experiences of my life.

I discovered that my new friend had been a professor at an eastern college. After his wife of 40 years died, he decided to pack up and move west. As he put it, he missed her terribly, but figured that he could either wait to die or face full-on the new life that lay before him. So he came to San Diego and, at age 75, had learned to surf. He learned the rhythms of the ocean, and it had become his sanctuary.

"The measure of a person is not the number of people who serve him, but the number of people he serves."

— *Unknown*

Now, over a decade later, he had developed some health problems and could no longer surf, but he still visited his old friend, the ocean, every day. He would spend hours people-watching and listening to the rhythm of the waves. He cherished each day, having found the satisfaction in life that eludes so many of us.

I asked him why he approached me. "Why not?" he said. "You seemed like an interesting person — though so do a lot of people on the beach. Maybe you would have turned out to be a complete slug. That would've been fine, too. Who knows? You could have been the most amazing person I've ever met. Either way, you never know until you take the time to find out."

After all these years, the old professor was still teaching, and I had the benefit of being, on that day at least, his only student. And the lesson he taught me — about taking the time to look beneath the surface — has stuck with me ever since.

He also taught me about how even the smallest pebbles, like one man passing the time of day with another, can have dramatic ripples. Those few hours with the old professor were the most memorable experience I had during my trip, and his words have stayed with me ever since. He helped change the way I look at the world, at myself, at the people in my life. Because he took the time to touch my life, I've had the opportunity — and the will — to impact others.

> **"Kindness is a hard thing to give away. It keeps coming back to the giver."**
> — *Unknown*

2. ***Ripples bounce back to us.*** Remember how the ripples in a pond hit the shore and are reflected back? That's true in our relationships as well. We may not know when or how, but our actions return to us. Call it karma if you want, but I've seen it happen time and time again.

I once helped the husband of a business acquaintance land a position with a new company. I didn't "get" him the job, mind you. I just made him aware of an opportunity, made a phone call or two, and he did the rest. But he was so grateful for my help that he later sent quite a bit of business my way. His wife, too, became a conduit for tens of thousands of dollars of referrals! All because I listened diligently, gave the matter a little thought, and spent a few minutes helping make a connection.

The lesson here is to be aware of your actions, even the little ones. Treat people badly or callously and it could come back to bite you in the rear. Treat them with respect and consideration and somehow, somewhere that positive energy will benefit you as well.

3. *Ripples continue long after we can no longer see them*. My knowledge of science is pretty limited, and it's influenced probably way too much by old Star Trek episodes. But something I always thought was pretty fantastic was the idea that energy can't be created or destroyed. It can change shape and form, but it can never cease to exist.

So although the energy that causes the ripples in that pond has spread so thin that we can't see it any more, we know that it's still there, still moving, still having a subtle impact. That's true of the relationships we form as well. The lessons I learned from the old San Diego professor I've passed along to others in my life, who have in some way passed them to still others. The ripples keep moving.

Shortly after moving to Waco, Texas from Albuquerque, New Mexico several years ago, I landed a huge account for my new company. Other salespeople had tried for years to win the business, but couldn't get past the gatekeeper. I did because I called early one morning before she was at her desk, reached the decision maker and scheduled an appointment.

Meeting with James a few weeks later, we discovered a mutual interest in soccer and baseball that helped transform a business relationship into a personal friendship. He noticed that I'd discovered a beautiful young employee of his and helped me (nervously) make contact with her. A year later I married Kathy, the girl whose smile had frozen me in my tracks, and today we have two amazing sons: Zachary (six and a half now) and Joshua (two).

James and I later became partners in a Xerox distributorship, by the way, and remain close friends even after its sale. Although I can't predict how, I'm sure we'll both continue to impact each others' lives many times in the years to come.

Obviously, Kathy and I have produced a lot of ripples as well, none so important as our sons. Through them, our influence will continue to impact others long after we're gone. And all because I chose to make a certain phone call at a certain time on a certain morning, and then made a connection with certain people!

The Business of Ripples

Ripples, like relationships, obviously aren't restricted simply to our personal lives. Successful businesses are built on mutually beneficial relationships: with employees, with vendors and suppliers, with distributors, and ultimately with clients and customers.

At a fundamental level, just doing business with integrity, fairness and honesty will create positive ripples. Customers will respect you, probably buy your products or use your services again, and even refer you to friends and family. Needless to say, that can translate into long-term customers and increased business.

> **At a fundamental level, just doing business with integrity, fairness and honesty will create positive ripples.**

But I want to encourage you to take it a few steps further. The fact is, we expect a fair price and decent service. Sure, we've all become a little more cynical and tempered our expectations a little these days, but we still have a pretty clear notion of what constitutes a bare minimum. Companies that meet that minimum are candidates for our future business, companies that don't become the subjects of irate e-mails to our friends and happy hour story swapping.

I find it interesting that studies have shown that people will share accounts of a bad customer experience with three or four times as many people as they will a good one. Human nature being what it is, I guess we all enjoy dishing dirt more than handing out compliments. But does it also mean that A) negative ripple effects are very real and can do tremendous damage and B) that we have to work harder to generate a positive business ripple effect?

To the first question, an emphatic yes! The ripple effect is based on the idea that actions have consequences. Some are intentional, some aren't. Some you can predict, some take on a life of their own. I've seen plenty of examples of how positive, selfless actions reap tremendous rewards for the doer — but I've seen just as many incidents where bad or thoughtless behavior came back to haunt a person. Cheat a customer and you'll begin to develop a reputation as a dishonest company; cheat enough customers and your professional days are numbered. Word gets around.

And it's not just actively trying to harm your customers that will cause negative ripples. Missed deadlines, wrong advice, failing to listen to client needs, disinterest, distraction — all those can be sometimes rationalized away with perfectly valid-sounding excuses. But even sins of omission can kill in today's business world. And if the person you disappointed tells eight or nine people, well, the ripples can spread pretty fast.

But is it harder to create positive ripples? I don't think so. In my experience, it's sometimes fairly small investments of time or money that pay off big time. People often respond better to the unexpected, even spontaneous gesture than the pre-planned, policy- or procedure-driven one.

Case in point: a commercial airline pilot flying one night from San Diego to Seattle bought, on a whim, Krispy Kreme donuts for everyone on board. When he announced it over the intercom, passengers gasped and broke into applause. "Never in my 17 years of flying for this company have I experienced a more appreciative and happier group of people," he later wrote to the Krispy Kreme company.

Think about all the goodwill he created for less than $50! Don't you think those passengers all told family, friends and co-workers? Don't you think they'll be willing — even eager — to fly that airline again? What a tremendous ripple effect that pilot created, just by being thoughtful. It cost him only a little time and money, but I'd be willing to bet he won his airline some customers for life, as well as some terrific grassroots PR.

It's those kinds of gestures — unexpected, considerate and selfless — that create customer evangelists willing to sing your praises to whoever will listen. It's like creating an unofficial, unpaid but highly effective salesforce. Think of the possibilities!

And, of course, it's not just our clients and customers we should be treating this way. Our internal clients — employees, co-workers and vendors — are just as important. Take the time to care about them and they'll walk through walls to bring you business. Treat them like disposable cogs in your business machine and they're likely to privately advise friends and acquaintances to shop elsewhere. Who knows where their ripples will end up?

Ron Willingham, the creator of the Integrity Selling system, talks a lot about what he calls the "law of reciprocity." This commonsense maxim says that any time you do something nice for someone, they unconsciously feel indebted to you and want to do something to pay you back: take you out to dinner, place an order, give you a referral, etc.

The law of reciprocity really helps drive positive ripple effects. In my own experience, I've helped plenty of business acquaintances, clients, colleagues and peers. I've referred them to others, introduced them to people who could really help their business, tracked down job opportunities, or in some way have gone above and beyond what they hired me to do. In offering that assistance, I didn't have any devious goals in mind or any vious goals in mind or any

> **All of us share a myriad of fluid, constantly changing connections, and the energy that flows through those connections is one of the most powerful forces on the planet.**

predisposed sense of how helping them would help me. It just seemed, in each situation, like the right thing to do. In most cases, it didn't cost me anything or take a lot of time.

What's amazing, though, is that helping them *did* help me. The people I've assisted have "repaid" me many times over: hundreds of thousands of dollars of referrals, introductions to vital contacts, and the creation of lucrative business alliances. My willingness to lend a hand when needed inspired them to find ways to benefit me.

Anyone who's been in business knows that referrals are more effective than advertising, and that's it's cheaper to keep an existing customer than to win over a new one. I'm here to tell you that adopting a ripple-oriented business mindset will both increase the number and quality of your referrals and strengthen your client relationships.

The Ripple Philosophy

Think about everything good in your life and your work. How much of it is really accidental? How much is the direct or indirect result of decisions you made and actions you took, maybe even years ago? Take the time to trace the chain of events that led you to your spouse, your job, your friends. Can you see the pattern?

All of us share a myriad of fluid, constantly changing connections, and the energy that flows through those connections is one of the most powerful forces on the planet. Recognizing that is one thing. Learn to harness it, and you've taken some big strides on the path to professional success and personal fulfillment.

Before you read any further, I want to make three points. First, the ripple effect is based on *actions*. Simply reading and reflecting on it won't change your life. Putting it into practice, I believe, will.

Second, maximizing the ripple effect in your life requires *conscious effort*. True, we make ripples all the time, whether we intend to or not. But, only by consciously setting positive ripples into motion, can we really get the most out of our relationships.

Third, creating beneficial ripples must become a *habit*. The opportunities to create ripples are constantly before us, but unless we've adopted ripple-oriented habits, we'll probably let too many of those chances slip by.

There's nothing particularly complicated about the principles the ripple effect is based upon. This isn't rocket science. But just because it's simple doesn't mean it's always easy. There will be a lot of times when you'll be tempted to fall back into old, self-centered ways of thinking. That's OK. It takes time to adjust our mindsets, expectations and habits. Don't let that keep you from trying, though. The rewards are worth it!

Points to Ponder

- The most powerful, the most successful, the most satis-fying accomplishments in both your life and your business result from the relationships you form with the people in your world.

- Those relationships are formed and influenced by a chain of consequence-bearing actions, each of which spawns new actions and new consequences — like the ripples created by a stone thrown into a pond.

- Ripples can be caused by even the smallest pebble, they bounce back to their origin, and they continue long after we can see them.

- Relationship-oriented ripples influence both our personal and professional success.

- To maximize the ripple effect in your life, you must take action, use it consciously and make it a habit.

Ripple Exercises

- Identify ripples others created that have significantly impacted your personal or professional life. How have ripples you've created in the past helped others?

- Make it a habit to consciously create at least three positive ripples for people this week . . . and every week.

Through the 18th century, ships' bottoms were coated with tar to protect them from being eaten by tiny molluscs that thrived in tropical waters. Unfortunately for the British, four-fifths of their tar supply came from the pine forests of the New World — which were largely closed to them after the American Revolution.

An impoverished Scottish nobleman, Archibald Cochrane, began experimenting with a means of extracting tar from coal. Once he accidentally let the pressure in a kiln rise beyond normal limits, and the kiln exploded. Cochrane noticed the resulting vapors ignited and burned brightly for a short time.

Cochrane mentioned the phenomenon in passing to an acquaintance, James Watt, who was also the inventor of the steam engine. Watt in turn mentioned it to a young man named William Murdock, who managed one of his steam engine factories. Murdock experimented with the odd gas, eventually using it to light one of his factories. By 1820, Britain's major towns and cities were all illuminated by gaslight.

Thanks to the new artificial light, streets became safer, factory production increased, literacy levels and book sales rose, and the industrial revolution reached full swing.

Archibald Cochrane, who had set all this in motion, perfected his tar extraction — only to find that the Admiralty had switched to sheathing ships' bottoms with copper. He died penniless in a Paris slum in 1831. Ironically, in the same city and the same year, one of his relatives also died, leaving him a fortune. Neither knew the other's whereabouts.

2 | RELATIONSHIP BUILDING FOR NON-PEOPLE PEOPLE

Understanding others better by understanding yourself better

It was my first day of kindergarten, and I was almost late. I remember getting to school just before class started and seeing all the other kids — whose mothers apparently didn't have some sort of curling iron malfunction — already forming up in little groups, playing with some classroom toys and laughing with each other.

I was by nature a shy little boy, so instead of walking right up to one of the groups I sort of hung back, watching, unsure of what to do. And as I waited, I saw something that's stuck with me ever since. The first thing I learned from kindergarten, as it turns out, I learned before class even started.

> "Lots of people want to ride with you in the limo, but what you want is someone who will take the bus with you when the limo breaks down."
>
> — *Oprah Winfrey*

One boy in particular was the center of attention. He was playing with this huge bright red toy fire engine — by far the best toy in the room. And a whole group of kids was just standing around: watching him, laughing at his antics, trying to get his attention, angling to be his friend.

Years later, I wondered: what if I'd been the first one to arrive, and had pulled the fire engine out of the toy box instead of him? Would I have been the center of attention? Would I have become the most popular boy in the room? Would my shyness have evaporated? Was it timing — or something else?

Mavens and Relaters and Evangelists . . . Oh My!

Humans have been trying to figure each other out pretty much from the beginning. The ancient Greeks may have been the first to categorize individual personalities into broad types: choleric, sanguine, phlegmatic, melancholic. For them, these types were innate and biological, corresponding to some predominant "humor" in your body. People were predisposed, they believed, to certain behaviors: phlegmatics were calm and unemotional, sanguine people were passionate and courageous, cholerics were irritable and hot-tempered, and melancholics were prone to depression and despondency.

The Greek model, with minor modifications, was the standard for nearly 2500 years. But with the advent of the more formal, scientific study of human psychology and psychiatry in the early 20th century, more and more behavior types were developed. Whereas the Greek model was rooted in nature (how we were born), most of the modern models focus more on nurture (how we were raised).

Now there are dozens (maybe even hundreds!) of competing and complimentary models, everything from the 16 personality types of the Myers-Briggs test to the four DISC types to the four buyer styles of the Integrity Selling system. Some models even categorize you based on what colors you prefer!

Used properly, personality profiles can be valuable tools for better learning about both ourselves and others. It's not about pigeon-holing or stereotyping people. It's about more systemically understanding — and appreciating — our similarities and differences. Understanding creates empathy, and empathy helps build relationships.

> "Sometimes you have to get to know someone really well to realize you're really strangers."
>
> — Mary Tyler Moore

But although nearly all of these models offer some interesting insights, too many of them are unwieldy and impractical for the layperson to understand and utilize. Most of us can't subject clients and acquaintances to lengthy personal questionnaires to determine where on the personality spectrum they fall. We need something powerful, but simple.

That's why I was thrilled to see *The Human Fabric*, written by my friend, Bijoy Goswami. Bijoy's the first to tell you that his categorization scheme, the MRE framework, helps refine some other models. Most importantly, besides just identifying different personality types, Bijoy devotes a lot of time to discussing how they relate to each other.

> **"Human behavior flows from three main sources: desire, emotion and knowledge."**
>
> — *Plato*

The MRE model divides people into Mavens, Relaters and Evangelists.

Mavens are motivated by the quest for knowledge. They want to create order by intellectually connecting the dots. They love information and details, and often seem to have single-track minds. Not surprisingly, they make terrific consultants, engineers and computer programmers. Often they have high IQs but a low EQs (Emotional Quotient). They may seem socially challenged — although they like to collaborate with other mavens to solve problems, they generally dislike small talk and person-to-person interaction. They love the Internet! At their best, they value a two-way exchange of knowledge and enjoy using their knowledge to help others.

Relaters are motivated by the need to form and preserve relationships. (It probably won't surprise you to learn that I'm a Relater!) They are usually the ones we mean when we talk about someone being a "people person." Relaters are nurturers, usually empathic, intuitive and patient. They care about the people they know and want to stay current on what's happening in the lives of their social network. Relaters don't necessarily know a lot of people (although it's a good bet they do), but the relationships they form are often deep and lasting. Strong Relaters may develop into **Connectors**, who *actively* seek to create new, mutually beneficial relationships among the people they know.

Evangelists are action-oriented. Persuasive and energetic, they're natural doers. Their favorite word is "yes!" For them, everything must have a purpose — and that applies both to *what* they know and *who* they know. Evangelists have a cause, and everything they do is designed to achieve or further it. They are effective communicators regardless of the medium, and are usually good at communicating complex ideas simply. Bijoy is a strong Evangelist, which is one of reasons why I think he's able to explain things so well in his book.

Can't We All Just Get Along?

After reading those descriptions, you've probably recognized yourself and those close to you as either a Maven, a Relater or an Evangelist. Of course, as Bijoy reminds us in *The Human Fabric*, we're really more complicated than just one type. We're usually blends of two of the three — I'm mostly a Relater, but I've got some Evangelist in me, too.

And don't assume that I don't like gadgets just because I'm not a Maven. I do. But my core motivation isn't acquiring knowledge; it's building relationships and encouraging you good people to do the same.

Since this is a book about relationship-building, some of you skeptical-minded Mavens may be wondering what you're doing here. After all, relationships are for, well, Relaters! And you Evangelists, you're probably looking at your watches — after all, you've got things to do and places to be, right? At least the Relaters are interested . . .

Actually, the point of this book is that relationships aren't just for Relaters! Relationships matter, maybe more than you realize. They matter both for what they are and for what they can accomplish. All of us — Mavens, Relaters, Evangelists — maximize our skills when they are blended with the skills of others. Thanks to various combinations of the three personality styles, ideas are developed, problems solved and needs identified. Before that can happen, we have to be able to relate to each other in a positive, sustainable fashion.

There are practical business reasons to make the conceptual leap as well. Business is all about relationships: relationships between you and your customers; relationships between you and your employees, colleagues and superiors; relationships between you and your vendors; and relationships between you and a crowd of other people who in some form or fashion have dealings with your company. Even if you're not in the sales department, you're still coming into contact every day with people who to some extent judge your company on your behavior.

And thanks to the relationship ripple effect, you're not just influenc-

> **Don't think for a second that it's only the sales and marketing folks who are shaping public opinion about your company. Everyone is, whether they intend to or not.**

ing those people. You're influencing their friends, families, colleagues, customers, clients, associates, acquaintances and employees. And it doesn't stop there, of course.

I think one of the more interesting quirks of human behavior is our tendency to tell about three times as many people about a negative experience as we do a positive one. If you make a lousy impression on someone or provide substandard service, odds are good that they in turn will tell seven to 12 people about it. Talk about a ripple effect!

Ever had a nice meal disrupted by a couple of loudmouth jerks at the next table? If they're both wearing company shirts, don't you tend to downgrade the firm in your mental ledger? I do. Almost involuntarily, I say to myself, "Any company that would hire these bozos probably isn't worth doing business with." By the same token, if a friend of a friend tells you at a party how miserable it is to work for Company X and how badly the owners treat their employees, don't you automatically think, "If they treat their own people this way, how can I trust them to treat me well as a customer?"

So don't think for a second that it's only the sales and marketing folks who are shaping public opinion about your company. Everyone is, whether they intend to or not. That's just the way ripples work.

I don't want to transform you Mavens into happy-hour-haunting power-networkers. I don't want you Evangelists to exchange your to-do lists for diaries. As Bijoy points out, we achieve our potential by recognizing and developing our gifts, not trying to emulate others' gifts. No matter how hard you try, Mavens and Evangelists, you'll never be Relaters.

But that doesn't mean you can't learn to relate better. In fact, I believe by doing so, you'll learn more (Mavens) and accomplish more (Evangelists) than you would have alone. And for you Relaters, I want you to take the next steps towards becoming Connectors. I want you to become more conscious about how you use your talent to better your life and the lives of those around you.

Finding Your Way

In *The Human Fabric*, Bijoy advises his readers to *discover* their core type, *deepen* their understanding of themselves and their gifts, ally with a complementary (not identical!) "*dance*" partner to combine the best of two types, and then *do it over* again. Keeping that in mind, let's take a look at a few practical ways Mavens and Evangelists can learn to relate, and how Relaters can develop their relational skills.

1. Practice putting people first. Too often, idea-focused Mavens are bored by flesh-and-blood people. Evangelists, meanwhile, are tempted to see others simply as a means to an end. Both groups need an occasional empathic jolt so they can see the world through others' eyes. In advocating a people-first philosophy, I'm definitely not talking about a schmooze-first mentality, or a small-talk mentality, or even a sales mentality. What I am talking about is treating other people as people — not as prospects or obstacles or consumers or any one of a thousand different labels we slap onto others every day.

Mavens and Evangelists, remind yourselves that everyone you encounter is a unique individual, with unique hopes, dreams, needs, talents and backgrounds. Curb your impulse to stereotype or dismiss them. If you can do that, it won't be long before you find some common connection. Maybe you grew up in the same town, or your brother once dated her sister, or you're both Chicago Bears fans, or you both love scuba diving. Whatever it is, once you've found that bond, you're already well on your way to establishing a positive relationship.

A friend of mine experienced the power of this people-first approach in a truly dramatic fashion. Mike's boss was a real office tyrant. He regularly berated his managers in front of the whole staff, constantly found fault and rarely gave out compliments. Mike absolutely dreaded going to work, and began seriously contemplating a job change.

Nor was he alone. His co-workers were just as miserable as he was, and as company morale sank lower it began to affect customer service. And, naturally, that just made Mike's boss come down even harder on everyone.

When Mike told me about his predicament, I asked him what he knew about his boss as a person. Not much, he admitted. I asked him to visualize his boss's office. Were there any awards, pictures or souvenirs? Mike thought he remembered seeing a picture of who he assumed were the man's wife and young son. Since Mike had just become a father himself, it seemed that there might be the beginnings of a connection here.

So I challenged Mike to ask about the photo the next time he found himself in the man's office. The results were pretty amazing.

The next day Mike went in to ask a question, which — as had become the norm — prompted a verbal tirade. During a pause, though, Mike said, "You're right, I should have known that. Hey, I guess I've never noticed the picture of your wife and son before. How old is he?"

You could have heard a pin drop. Finally, the boss said softly, "That's Billy. He's five —or at least he was when that picture was taken."

"Well, he's a fine-looking boy," Mike said.

Suddenly, Mike's boss began sobbing. "Billy's mom took him away from me," he said. "She was having an affair and left in the middle of the night. I haven't seen or heard from them in over two years."

Mike instantly felt a stab of pain for the man. He was no longer an overbearing jerk, just a grieving father desperately longing for his young son. Mike sat down and just listened. For nearly an hour, his boss poured his heart out. He had been so consumed with his own career that he'd never had an inkling that his wife was cheating on him until he read her "Dear John" note. He felt he had failed as a husband and as a father, and all he wanted was the chance to set things right with his son.

And that, his boss confessed, was why he was so hard on everyone in the office. His work was the only thing he had left. But since he blamed it for his failed marriage and a lost relationship with his son, he resented it as well. So he poured all his anger, frustration and effort into running an efficient department.

He asked Mike if everyone there hated him. Mike, truthfully if somewhat bluntly, told him yes. And finally the two men talked about the problems in the office — without anger, without defensiveness and without recrimination.

That emotional conversation marked a turning point for the office. The boss, finally aware of what he was doing and how he was treating his employees, stopped his destructive behavior. He didn't become perfect (this wasn't quite an Ebenezer Scrooge makeover), but he was orders of magnitude better than he used to be.

Just goes to show what can happen when you adopt a people-first mentality. Once Mike was able to see his boss as a person (and vice versa), they were able to put aside their antagonism and build the foundation for a productive, long-term relationship.

> "All the discontented people I know are trying to be something they are not, to do something they cannot do."
>
> — David Graydon

2. *Be sincere.* If you're a Maven or an Evangelist, don't try to act like a Relater. It will feel forced to you and seem insincere to the person you're dealing with. This goes for Relaters, too — you may think you have to supplement your natural gift with some kind of trick. Too many sales and relationship "how to" books (and tapes, vid-

eos and seminars) treat personal interaction as some sort of game, or contest, or war. Your "objective" is getting a sale or getting a date or whatever, and to do that you're encouraged to outsmart, outtalk and outmaneuver the other person.

In my experience, that's bad for business and potentially deadly when it comes to building relationships. If the person you're speaking with gets the idea that the sale is all that matters to you, that your buddy-buddy act is just that — well, I wouldn't spend that commission in advance if I were you.

Earlier this year I experienced this phenomenon firsthand. I was shopping for a new car, and went to a big, well-established dealership. Immediately a slick-looking salesman came over, smiled broadly, and asked me what I was looking for. I told him the make and model I'd had in mind.

He suddenly looked very serious. "I'll be frank with you, Steve," he said. "That's a very good vehicle. But it's not the absolute safest vehicle on the market. And don't you want your family to be safe?"

He steered me over to one of their top-of-the-line SUVs and began extolling its virtues. "This is what I drive," he said. "I wouldn't trust anything else to protect my family. What about you?"

The guy was a little too practiced, a little too smarmy — a Relater gone over to the Dark Side. I made my excuses and thanked him for his time. As I was leaving I overheard him tell a co-worker that he was going to take his lunch break. Curious, I got into my car, waited a few minutes and (you guessed it) saw him get into a very different vehicle than the SUV he was trying to push on me.

First his sincerity seemed a little suspect. Now his credibility was completely shot. Do you think I bought a car from him? Of course not. Do you think I'd ever buy a car from that dealership? No. Will I warn my friends and family to take their business elsewhere as well? You bet.

Despite the sales success I have achieved, I am not a particularly good salesman. Really! What I am good at is being an advisor, a problem solver and invariably a friend. That sincere desire to help has transformed many of my clients over the years into friends, which has been a lot more satisfying than the commissions I've earned or the bonuses I've achieved. That, I think, has been the truest measure of success.

Mavens, you're terrific problem solvers. Put that skill at the disposal of others: co-workers, friends, clients, etc. Evangelists, you know how to get things done. That can be a big help for someone not a natural go-getter. Relaters, follow your intuition and empathy, not some artificial formula.

Sincerity — or the lack of it — matters. Tips, tricks and tactics can't match an honest interest and a sincere desire to help find a mutually satisfying solution for your customer's needs. Relationship building isn't about being clever. It's about being real.

3. Ask questions and learn to listen to the answers. Uncomfortable around new people, Mavens? Here's an invaluable bit of advice for you: ask questions. Most folks love talking about themselves, their family, their business, their hobbies — you name it. Just keep them talking and you'll see how effortless it can be. Chances are that they'll even like you more because you displayed an interest in them! And while they're telling you all this great information, there's an excellent possibility your shyness will evaporate as you discover a mutual friend, hobby or interest.

Evangelists are notorious for talking too much, for being more interested in what *they* have to say than in what anyone else has to say. They tend to interrupt — a lot. So, Evangelists, remember this: some of history's great conversationalists were known more for their consummate listening skills than their witty banter. And active listening really is a skill. The next time you're talking with a new person, practice 1) *listening* to what they're saying and 2) *asking* follow-up questions. The questions don't have to be particularly insightful or clever. Just let the person know you've heard what they said and you're interested in learning more. And don't interrupt! I think you'll be surprised how quickly their barriers go down, and how much they'll warm up to you.

4. Find the right dance partner(s). I love Bijoy's emphasis on discovering and developing partnerships with other core personality types. Mavens and Evangelists make particularly powerful pairings: think about Apple Computer's Steve Jobs (Evangelist) and Steve Wozniak (Maven) or Microsoft's Bill Gates (Evangelist) and Paul Allen (Maven).

But other pairings can be productive, too. Relaters and Evangelists can combine to make their world a better, kinder, nicer place to live. Mavens and Relaters can make technology more user-focused and user-friendly.

Ideally, I think you should work to find more than one dance partner. Mavens and Evangelists, you're not naturally good at relating, so ally yourself with one or more Relaters

> "Soulmates are people who bring out the best in you. They are not perfect, but are always perfect for you."
>
> — *Unknown*

and let them help you build relationships. Relaters and Evangelists, develop Mavens as advisors and brain trusts. Mavens and Relaters, remember that Evangelists are key to taking your dreams and your knowledge and transforming them into reality.

Also, don't pre-judge people. There are some terrific Relaters who aren't Fortune 500 execs or champion salespeople. Consider my barber, John, who is one of the best Relaters I know.

John is a terrific conversationalist with an amazing memory, and just has a knack for making people feel comfortable. Not surprisingly, he's also a great listener, and he's always looking for ways to be a better resource for his clients. He also knows an enormous number of people, some of them very influential.

Once, another of John's regulars struck up a conversation with me as we were waiting. The man was attempting to launch a new business, and desperately needed a connection to the city council. From overhearing some of my conversations with John, he knew I was fairly well-connected, so he began picking my brain for advice.

We chatted for about 10 minutes, and while I was able to give him some good general tips, I knew John was a potentially far better resource. He knew most of Austin's politicians — heck, most of them were clients! So I suggested that he tell John what he was trying to accomplish and ask his advice.

"You must be kidding!" the man laughed. "John's just a barber. He cuts hair for a living. What could he possibly know about business?"

Taken aback, I didn't say a word. I was shocked by his elitism. A few awkward minutes passed. "Seriously," he said, somewhat apologetically, "John's a great guy, but I doubt he'd even grasp the concept. I need someone who understands business."

> **"Great opportunities come to all, but many do not know they have met them."**
>
> — *Albert E. Dunning*

Just then it was my turn in the barber's chair. Knowing that my new acquaintance was listening to our conversation, I casually asked John about his friends on the council. Laughing, he told me some of the funny stories that had happened over the years. Glancing over at the businessman, I asked John about the one person this guy needed to meet more than any other. John said that they'd been friends for a long, long time, and they often met for coffee on his day off. Out of the corner of my eye, I could see the businessman squirming.

As I left, I stopped by his chair and said softly, "Never judge a book by its cover." Red-faced, he simply shook his head.

So get out there and build relationships! Don't just assume someone isn't worth getting to know — try it and see. You never know where the ripples you make might end up.

5. *Practice, practice, practice*. I know that putting yourself in a position to meet new people can be hard. I still get sweaty palms and knots in my stomach when I have to speak to a group, or when I'm in a strange new situation. The difference for me now is that those feelings disappear a lot quicker.

I know it's always risky, putting yourself out there. What if they think I'm an idiot? What if they don't like me? What if I have something on my collar? What if I make a fool of myself?

I won't lie to you — encounters aren't always going to go smoothly. But odds are there will be more good than bad, and even the bad will teach you something positive. Want proof? Let me tell you about my very first sales call.

I was 18 and green as could be. I'd gotten a job as a sales-man for an office machine company more out of desperation than anything else, since I needed money to help pay for college and a girlfriend with expensive tastes.

The owner of the company was a great guy, and I learned a lot about the office machine and office supply business from him. Unfortunately, though, he wasn't a particularly good teacher when it came to the art and science of making sales calls. He basi-cally just handed me a stack of product information and shooed me out of the office with the encouraging words, "OK, now go sell something!"

Dumb kid that I was, I didn't know any better. Bright and eager and armed with a pile of four-color brochures, I smiled like a kid in a candy store as I surveyed all the office buildings in my new territory. I could sense that there was a fortune in potential sales there, a fortune that was mine for the taking. I gave myself a little pep talk about how easy this was going to be.

My triumphant mood was dampened only slightly as I marched up to the first building and saw the NO SOLICITING sign on the door. "Well," I reasoned with dubious logic, "I'm sure that doesn't apply to me. I'm not selling cookies here. I've got high-end office equipment, and everyone needs that."

So I opened the door and walked over to a building di-rectory. And I did what no salesperson should ever do: I started adding up all the money I was going to make. There were about 20 companies in the building, and I figured that if I sold each a $10,000 copier . . . well, images of sports cars and Rolexes started spinning through my 18-year-old mind. I was the king of sales, and life was good.

Smiling, I walked into the first office. The receptionist, a pleasant-looking middle-aged woman, looked up smiling from her desk . . . and saw my armload of brochures. Her welcoming smile vanished instantly, replaced by a grim scowl and dark stare. "Yes?" she said in a tone that froze my marrow.

"Uh . . . um," I stammered. Suddenly, the lights in the room seemed to dim. The only thing I could see, almost as though she was lit up by a spotlight, was the receptionist.

"Well, what can I do for you?" she sneered. I couldn't answer. I couldn't think. I just wanted to turn and run, but it felt like my feet were stuck to the black tile floor. I felt faint, my mouth was desert-dry and my heart was beating so hard I was surprised it didn't pop right out of my chest. If it had, I'm sure the creature that had been the receptionist would have eaten it on the spot.

"Look, are you lost or something?" she asked in exasperation. I felt like a rabbit caught in a trap. Vaguely I moved my head in a motion she took to mean yes.

"Oh," she said, smiling sweetly again. The evil witch of the west was gone, replaced by the warm, pleasant woman I'd seen when I first walked in. "For a minute there I thought you were selling something. I saw you carrying brochures and thought you were just another salesman."

Just another salesman. "No!" I wanted to shout. "I'm not just another salesman. I am *the* salesman!" But the words wouldn't come. Instead, I mumbled something about this not being my brother's office and retreated as fast as my legs would carry me.

Hard to believe anything positive came out of that experience, right? And yet it showed me the importance of training, of proper planning — and of relationships. I saw firsthand the pitfalls of cold calling, and how different it would have been if I'd already had an advocate in that office. As humiliating and downright frightening as that experience was, it helped set me on a better path.

Discomfort Zones

I'm sure you've heard of "comfort zones," the places and situations where we feel at ease. Get out of them! Growth comes through facing, and overcoming, new challenges. Stay in your comfort zone and you'll stagnate.

Mavens, Relaters, Evangelists — make a conscious effort to use your natural gifts to make positive ripples. If your forte is action, make it "other-focused action." If it's knowledge, use the knowledge to help others. And if your strength is relating to people, take the time to connect others. I'm counting on you to draw those Mavens out of their shell and help direct Evangelists' energy towards positive goals. Talk to people, whether it's at networking functions or in your neighborhood coffee shop. Make the effort to reach out to people, to find those common connections, to build those new relationships.

> **What's the opportunity cost of not reaching out to the people you encounter? Lost dreams, lost knowledge, lost successes, lost profits, lost love, lost fulfillment.**

In a world that too often equates popularity with success and image with worth, it's hard for naturally shy folks to get out there and make ripples. And it's all too easy to focus on the risks. In business, we talk about "opportunity costs" — how taking one course of action precludes you from another. If, for example, you invest your money in one stock, it means that you couldn't invest those funds elsewhere. The trick is determining which course of action is most profitable. Too many lost opportunities and your company will likely be treading water at best.

What's the opportunity cost of not reaching out to the people you encounter? Lost dreams, lost knowledge, lost successes, lost profits, lost love, lost fulfillment. And what's the risk in doing so? The chance you might be embarrassed? I'll take that trade-off any day.

I know it can be tough. But better to try and fall short occasionally than to harbor a growing list of regrets that your life never turned out quite the way you envisioned it. The resources to make your dreams happen really are out there, surrounding you, if you'll just take the time — and summon the courage — to act.

Points to Ponder

- People can be categorized into three broad personality types: *Mavens, Relaters* and *Evangelists*.

- *Mavens* are motivated by the acquisition of knowledge. *Relaters* are motivated by the desire to understand people. *Evangelists* are motivated by the need for goal-oriented action.

- Mavens and Evangelists can never (and should never) try to be Relaters, but they can (and should) still understand the importance of relationships.

- Even a non-people person can develop relationship-building skills by trying to put people first, being sincere, asking questions (and learning to listen to the answers), finding the right personality "dance partner," and practicing, practicing, practicing.

- The risks of leaving your comfort zone to build relationships are less than the opportunity costs of *failing* to do so.

Ripple Exercises

- Identify whether you are a Maven, Relater or Evangelist. How do you know? What's your secondary type? Now do the same for some of the people in your life: family, friends, co-workers and employees.

- Identify three prospective "dance partners." What specific actions can you take this week to better connect with these people?

- Break out of your comfort zone this week by initiating contact with someone you don't know in a business or social setting. Consciously ask relationship-building questions and listen to the answers.

PART 2

Planning a Relationship Strategy

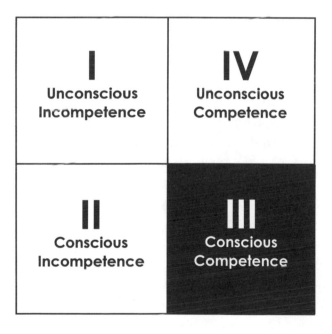

I	**IV**
Unconscious Incompetence	Unconscious Competence
II	**III**
Conscious Incompetence	Conscious Competence

In the late 1960s, psychologist Stanley Milgram tried to determine just how human beings are connected to each other. Do we lead isolated, autonomous lives? Or are we all part of some immense, interlocking web?

Milgram examined this "small world problem" by mailing 160 people in Omaha, Nebraska, each a packet. Inside the packet was the name and address of a Boston stockbroker. The recipients were instructed to write their name on the packet and send it on to a friend, family member or acquaintance they thought would get the packet closer to the stockbroker. They were prohibited, obviously, from simply sending it to the stockbroker directly.

As Malcolm Gladwell, author of The Tipping Point, *writes, "If you lived in Omaha and had a cousin outside of Boston, for example, you might send it to him, on the grounds that — even if your cousin did not himself know the stockbroker — he would be a lot more likely to be able to get to the stockbroker in two or three or four steps. The idea was that when the packet finally arrived at the stockbroker's house, Milgram could look at the list of all those whose hands it went through to get there an establish how closely connected someone chosen at random from one part of the country was to another person in another part of the country."*

Milgram's findings surprised him and gave us a new concept of how society works. He found that most of the letters reached the stockbroker in only five or six steps. In summing up the results, Milgram proposed that there were only six degrees of separation between any two people.

Milgram's experiment helped show how closely connected human beings really are — and how quickly ripples can travel through society.

------

3 | SIX DEGREES FROM SUCCESS
The art of leveraging relationships

Back in 1967, a professor named Stanley Milgram wrote an article for *Psychology Today* called "The Small World Problem." In the article, he detailed an experiment he had conducted on how to create a connection between two total strangers through a network of mutual acquaintances, friends and colleagues. Based on his results, he suggested that only "six degrees of separation" separated anyone from anyone else.

Since Milgram first proposed the theory, it's become something of a pop cultural fixture. Someone even developed a party game based on the concept. In "Six Degrees of Kevin Bacon," participants stretch their memories to connect actors and actresses to Kevin Bacon through a web of movie roles. The fewer the steps, the better. Let me say for the record: people who can do this consistently have waaay too much time on their hands.

That said, the six degrees of separation theory really is pretty amazing. Think about it — you're only five or six people away from finding anyone or anything we could ever want. Five or six people from knowing the head of a Fortune 500 company, your favorite movie star, or even the President of the United States! Talk about a ripple effect.

(By the way, Milgram's experiment also helps prove the existence of Connectors in our society. Of the 24 letters that reached the Massachusetts stockbroker at his home, 16 were given to him by the same person, a clothing merchant. The balance of the letters that reached him at the office were also delivered mostly by two men. In all, half of the letters that reached him did so through three men. As author Malcolm Gladwell writes in *The Tipping Point*, "Six degrees of separation doesn't mean that everyone is linked to everyone else in just six steps. It means that a very small number of people are linked to everyone else in a few steps, and the rest of us are linked to the world through those special few.")

I have long been fascinated by the power of a huge bandwidth of available contacts. Success, I discovered early on, isn't so much a function of *what* you know as it is *who* you know — and who knows you. As a business owner, that translates into who you *need* to know to be successful. The six degrees theory gives you a tool to make those connections happen.

I experienced the rush of the six degrees theory myself not long ago. While having lunch with a colleague, I mentioned something about how neat it would be to meet President George W. Bush. Turns out my friend had a friend who used to run and play golf with the President when he lived in Midland. The two remain friends and still speak fairly often. My score: three degrees of separation. Pretty cool.

"We cannot live only for ourselves. A thousand fibers connect us with our fellow men."

— Herman Melville

But that's not the end of it. I also have a good friend who attends the same church as the Bushes when they're in Austin. My friend and his wife even socialized with the President and Mrs. Bush when he was the Governor of Texas. They don't know him particularly well . . . but they are friends with another couple who have been lifelong friends of the Bushes and have even been to several White House functions. Again, just three degrees of connections separate me from the most powerful man on the planet. Imagine if I really got motivated to meet the President and had both sets of contacts working on my behalf. The odds of it actually happening go up considerably — far more than if I were to go it alone and try and meet him on my own.

And there's another interesting aspect to the situation. Even if I could, on my own somehow, arrange for a meeting with Mr. Bush, he'd likely treat me like any other anonymous private citi-

zen off the street. But if he
were to hear, from two different sources he trusts, that
this Steve Harper fella is a
good guy — well, I'd be

Having others vouch for me increases my credibility and helps build trust.

very surprised if that didn't alter how he perceived me. It might
very well stimulate his desire to meet me. Having others vouch
for me increases my credibility and helps build trust before I ever
meet the man.

Six Degrees of Business

While I've never put this to the test with President Bush, I
have seen it happen many times in my career, both for me and for
people I've worked with. The payoff can be quite amazing. What
you tend to find is that the person you're meeting already feels a
connection to you, and a lot of that early awkwardness and for-
mality can be dispensed with.

Since both sides are more relaxed, chances for building a
good rapport are put on the fast track. With some of those initial
barriers removed, you're in a much better position to make a sale,
win a contract or get a job. I built my sales career utilizing those
kinds of opportunities. Often they led to even bigger, more profitable sales — and ones that generally faced little if any competition.

Sometimes the benefits of making a connection like this
aren't immediately apparent. Shortly after moving to Austin, a
contact of mine at a local moving company brought up a problem
during a networking event. His company, which had primarily
focused on residential moves, was trying to break into the commercial moving business but was having trouble finding the right
approach.

As it turned out, I had a contact at a local property management company that was planning to move several tenants from
one of their older properties to a new building that was nearing
completion. So I suggested that the moving company strike up
a partnership with the management company. I mentioned what

a significant value I thought the property management company could offer to their tenants if the moving company offered a co-operative rate for all those moves. The moving company, meanwhile, would gain the needed entry into the commercial sector, with a well-known property management company and about 20 tenant companies as immediate clients.

I was able to connect the two businesses and help create a real win/win situation. The moving company gained instant credibility and a significant pop in revenue. The property management company, meanwhile, looked like heroes to their tenants by securing such favorable rates and terms. Everyone was happy.

As for me — well, I didn't get involved because I saw the prospect of any immediate personal gain. I never asked for, or even expected, a thing from my involvement. I was just helping a couple of colleagues solve two seemingly unconnected problems by making a connection. But as it turns out, both companies became clients of mine just a few months later, in no small part because of the trust and credibility I'd earned through my suggestion. My minimal investment of time and energy ultimately resulted in over $25,000 worth of direct business for me — more when you consider that the decision makers at both companies also became great referral sources.

What if you mobilized your web of contacts? How many people would benefit? How many connections could you make? The ripples might surprise you.

Ripples in Motion

We'll focus in Chapter Four on the pros and cons of formal business networking groups. But what we should learn from the six degrees of separation theory is that we're always networking, whether we realize it or not. And the results of that informal networking can be dramatic. The guy standing next to you in the elevator could be the inroad to a big account. The neighbor down the street could be the purchasing manager for a technology company about to hit it big.

Want to put this idea to the test? Spend three hours in a Starbucks and see how many interesting people you come across. The opportunity for meeting any number of influential people — for meeting people who know people who know people — is right there at your local coffee shop. You just have to be brave enough to take the initiative.

The problem is that we've all been conditioned to avoid the possibility of being rejected or looking stupid. Most of us are happy enough to talk if someone approaches us, but we don't have the nerve to make the first move. So we order our coffee, silently and quickly stir in our cream and sugar, and go about our business without making eye contact with anyone else. Too often we move through the world like sheep.

What's sad about that behavior is that it causes us to miss out on a whole world of possibilities, on the chance to meet a wide range of new and interesting

> **How many of us might be millionaires if we'd only had the courage to strike up conversations more often with strangers?**

people — people (or the people who know them) who might become outstanding personal and professional opportunities. How many of us might be millionaires if we'd only had the courage to strike up conversations more often with strangers? How many of us might have found friends, spouses, employers and employees? How much richer and more satisfying might our lives be?

No matter how you slice it, the potential payoff is worth the risk of saying "hi," don't you think? Take the plunge and attempt to start a conversation with five new people today. I'm confident you'll be surprised and impressed with the results.

Of course, most casual conversations don't begin with questions about what you do for a living. Usually we're more comfortable talking about some item of common interest, like the weather, sports or world events. But sooner or later the discussion turns to professional or personal matters, and suddenly the possibilities of this chance encounter are endless.

A couple words of advice: whenever possible, try to get contact information for the people you meet. Also try to find some sort of connection with them and add a mental note to your knowledge network. The connection could be as simple as the fact that they're looking for a new job or happen to like the Chicago Cubs. Whatever it is, chances are good that you'll eventually run across something related to that connection that might have some value to them. If the guy you just met is a Cubs fan and you see a tidbit on the Internet about a potential trade, send him the link to the news story. If you don't have his e-mail, this gives you a perfect excuse to call him up and ask for it in order to send him something of interest.

> "Goodwill is the mightiest practical force in the universe."
>
> — Charles F. Dole

The consideration that he sees you putting forth based on one or two limited conversations can make a big deposit in your emotional bank account with this guy. It is really rewarding to see the impact you can have on someone when you do something totally unexpected. They'll often jump through hoops to reciprocate — even if your act took comparatively little time or money — and that often turns into business, friendship or something more down the road.

Not Just for Business Anymore

Soon after my wife Kathy and I moved to a new subdivision, many of the neighborhood ladies stopped by to introduce themselves and invite Kathy to all sorts of community activities, including a hobby party. Kathy can be a little shy in new situations, so it meant a lot to both of us that our new neighbors took the initiative to reach out and establish a connection.

Even though she was a little hesitant to accept their invitation, she was reassured by the ladies' obvious sincerity and warmth. And sure enough, she had a terrific time. Everyone was very friendly and welcoming. She met a number of people that, had she not stepped beyond her immediate comfort zone, she would likely never have gotten to know or had the opportunity to interact with.

Beginning with that first hobby party, I watched Kathy

emerge from her shell. Her confidence grew as she took a more active role within our community and established a number of new friendships. Opened to some of the exciting opportunities suddenly available to her, she felt happier and more fulfilled.

What Kathy was doing, even if she didn't realize it at the time, was a kind of informal networking. The nature of networking is the development of contacts and the exchange of information with others. That party (and all the subsequent events) was a chance for Kathy to tell people a little bit about herself and to learn about others. Through this information exchange, the women were able to lay the groundwork for meaningful future contact.

Thanks to that party, Kathy met several ladies who shared similar interests, and they became fast friends. One of them was very active in the neighborhood association and became a terrific resource for us as new arrivals. She knew all the happenings, could tell us when to sign the kids up for swim lessons, who to call if the garbage hadn't been picked up, and when the next block party was scheduled. Other ladies, now that they knew who we were and where we lived, could keep their eyes peeled for any suspicious activity when we weren't home. Thanks to some proactive neighbors and one party, suddenly we had access to a whole network of community resources and information. Instead of being isolated as newcomers, we were connected to a wider world.

Any chance you get to put your best foot forward and meet people contains the seeds of a tremendous personal and professional payoff. Most people think of networking purely as a business activity. But the reality is that it is every bit as important in your personal life as well. Just consider the advantages of being able to call the computer expert down the street when your system crashes one evening, or knowing that a guy a block over has a plumbing snake that can unclog your kitchen sink.

Little things, maybe, but life is sure a lot less frustrating when you can plug into that kind of network. If some sort of need or problem suddenly arises, wouldn't you feel better knowing immediately who to call for help or advice? And wouldn't it be a comfort that these people would be inclined to deal with you fairly and honestly, and even go above and beyond to resolve your problem? I know I sleep a little better at night for having so many great resources literally a phone call away.

Setting Relationship Goals

Networking, whether formal or informal, connects you to who you need to know. But establishing that connection is only the first step. The goal is to build a mutually-beneficial relationship. To do that, it's helpful to ask some questions and set some goals.

1. Categorize the relationship. This can — and should — evolve over time, so it's not like you're pigeonholing someone into a category they'll never leave. Nor should this be some kind of coldly-calculated judgment about how to "use people." No, all this really means is that you need to determine some initial boundaries. Is this predominately personal or professional? Do you think this will likely remain a casual contact, or does it have the potential to become something more?

2. Determine if the relationship is worth developing. Again, that can be a tough determination to make up front, which is why it's important to categorize relationships to some extent. Maintaining a casual connection involves a much smaller investment of your time and energy than developing a close business ally. The payoff, though, can be amazing.

Here's a story from my own experience. My company was installing a new digital copier at a big law firm. To be safe, they requested that their third-party computer and network consultant be present to help work out any bugs that might arise. I remember feeling a little like I was in a showdown at the OK Corral. The consultant, Rick Cloud of Counselor Systems, clearly wasn't all that thrilled that we were risking mucking up his network by adding this new-fangled device.

I realized that Rick's continued opposition could really endanger the account, so I made a conscious effort to win him over. Since a technical debate was likely to become even more heated and adversarial (and one in which I was at a distinct disadvantage), I decided to try and shift the conversation. I asked him questions about his company, how long he'd been in business, and why he was drawn to that industry in the first place. Before long, a lot of those barriers I'd sensed had come down.

It ended up being a pretty good experience. Once we both realized the other was a good guy with the client's interests at heart, we were able to work together surprisingly well. Turns out our philosophies were very similar — something I never would have guessed when I first met him. At the end of the day, I actually referred Rick to another client of mine who was having some computer problems. We also swapped cards and promised to stay in touch.

> **"Make yourself necessary to somebody."**
> — *Ralph Waldo Emerson*

A lot of connections end there. But the more I thought about it, the more I realized what a powerful and natural alliance our two companies could form. I made the decision to develop that casual connection into something deeper. So I did what not enough businesspeople do. Instead of waiting for him to call me, I picked up the phone and asked Rick out to lunch.

That conversation became the first of many over the next several months. We shared information, suggestions and affirmations. We learned more about each other as individuals and as businessmen. We discovered common interests and shared goals and became good friends. Eventually, we were able to even implement a few joint deals, as well as refer clients to each other. Over the years, I'd estimate the value of the resulting business at several hundred thousand dollars.

I'd say that was definitely a relationship worth developing!

3. Establish trust first — work out the specifics later. Too often we want to jump ahead in a relationship — to get to the "good stuff." We forget that relationships are based on trust and comfort, and you can't rush those. If I'd started talking to Rick about how much business we could do together without first earning his trust, I'm certain that relationship would never have matured. Rick had dealt with a lot of salespeople and had learned from experience to be skeptical. It was only after he found out more about my background, my principles and me as a person that he lowered his guard.

Patience is vital in building any relationship. Don't get ahead of yourself. Before committing your business, your clients or your reputation, make every effort to discover the other person's character, and be sure they know yours.

4. Follow up. So many promising connections fail to develop because neither side makes an effort to follow up. If I hadn't asked Rick out to lunch, how likely is it that we would have become both friends and business allies? I'd say the odds would have been pretty low. Don't leave money on the table because you thought you were too busy or too shy to pursue the possibilities.

> **"Our worth is determined by the good deeds we *do*, rather than the fine emotions we *feel*."**
>
> — *Elias L. Magoon*

And keep in mind that one lunch, one phone call or one e-mail isn't enough. It's like the guy who says, "I tried networking last Thursday, and it didn't work!" Building relationships take time, energy and effort. Remember that.

5. The 80/20 Rule. You're probably familiar with some version of the 80/20 Rule: in sales, 20 percent of your clients provide 80 percent of your revenue. Accordingly, you should focus 80 percent of your marketing efforts on those top 20 percent.

The same is true in building networks. Probably 20 percent of your contacts will be responsible for 80 percent of your positive ripples. So you should spend 80 percent of your time, energy and effort reinforcing and developing those relationships. Cultivate the connectors in the groups you encounter — those are the folks who can create the most powerful and farthest-reaching ripples for you.

For casual contacts, the occasional e-mail or conversation at a networking event may be sufficient to sustain the connection. For more promising relationships, take the time to touch base regularly by phone and set up regular lunches, happy hours or dinners. And always look for little unexpected ways to deliver value and reinforce the relationship.

Thanks to the six degrees of separation, all of us have access to an unbelievable number of contacts. When I sat down and charted some of mine, I discovered connections that led to country music, cutting-edge cancer treatments, one of the largest financial management companies in the world and now, even the President of the United States! When you start breaking down who you know, and who *they* know, the possibilities of expanding your life and career increase exponentially.

So take the time to map out your various contacts and who you think your contacts know. Set some goals: meeting the mayor, or perhaps a local television personality or influential businessperson. Once you've determined who you want to meet, communicate it to all of your contacts and see what happens. Remember — nothing can happen until you share your goals with your network.

One other suggestion: do some reverse mapping and see who *you* know or have access to that could help one of your clients or contacts. Chances are you hold the key right now to unlocking a door of opportunity for someone. Do it once and they'll owe you one. Do it regularly and they could become your friend, advocate and resource for life!

Points to Ponder

- No more than six degrees separate you from anyone else.

- Whether we're aware of it or not, we're always networking.

- Learning to maximize, mobilize and effectively leverage our web of connections can have amazing results in both our personal and professional lives.

- When meeting new contacts, ask yourself first what kind of relationship opportunities are present, and if the relationship is worth developing. If it is, focus on building trust and following up on the initial meeting.

- For business relationships, focus 80 percent of your network building on the 20 percent of relationships most likely to yield positive results.

Ripple Exercise

- Using the Connector Model below, put the name of a friend, family member, co-worker or associate in the center circle.

- Now identify 5 people that might be able to help them personally or professionally. Determine whether they are predominantly Mavens, Relaters or Evangelists.

- Facilitate the connection by setting up face-to-face meetings between the center circle and each of the surrounding circles.

RELATIONSHIP CONNECTOR MODEL

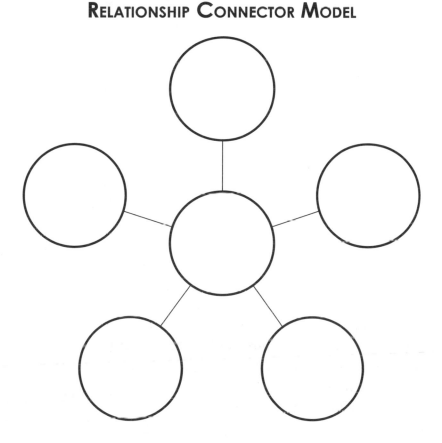

Ripple effects aren't always positive, but they are no less dramatic.

On January 27, 1967, three U.S. astronauts died when their Apollo 1 command module burst into flame during a routine launchpad test. Their deaths shocked the nation and forced NASA to re-examine some core procedures.

The fire was caused by a tiny spark in some damaged wires hidden from view under the astronauts' "couch." Aided by a small leak of flammable fumes from a nearby coolant pipe, the spark ignited some nylon webbing that had been installed to catch dropped equipment.

The atmosphere in the module was pure oxygen. In orbit, when the cabin pressure was only 5 psi, that posed no difficulties. But on the launchpad in Florida, slightly above sea-level, the cabin was pressurized to 16.7 psi. Pure oxygen is a fire risk even at low pressure; at 16.7 psi, the danger is frighteningly high. Somehow no one had realized that.

In that volatile environment, the spark that ignited the nylon webbing immediately spread out in a sheet of flame. Velcro wall fasteners, used excessively by the astronauts to secure loose objects in the weightlessness of space, exploded like they'd been doused in gasoline. Within seconds, the temperature in the module soared to 2,500 degrees Fahrenheit.

The astronauts' only chance was the escape hatch. But for reasons of weight, the hatch opened inward instead of outward as on earlier Mercury and Gemini capsules. The designers also considered it a safer design — the outward-opening hatch on Gus Grissom's Mercury flight may have prematurely blown while tossing in the sea after reentry, nearly drowning Grissom. The Apollo hatch would not do likewise.

Unfortunately, it was also unusable. The tremendous heat caused equally high pressure, and the hatch was sealed shut with thousands of pounds of force. In less than a minute, the three astronauts were dead.

One of them was Gus Grissom.

---

4 | NETWORKING FACT AND FICTION

Making the most of your opportunities

B usiness networking has become one of the hot trends in the last few years. There are networking breakfasts, networking lunches, networking happy hours and networking dinners. There are networking conferences, networking parties and, believe it or not, networking networks. And, of course, there are a bunch of books out there that offer you networking tips, tactics and techniques.

But for all its growing popularity, the question remains: does networking really increase sales? Or does all that eating out simply increase your waistline instead? Is networking for real, or just an excuse to put lunch, dinner or drinks on the old expense account?

"Everyone needs help from everyone."

— Bertolt Brecht

Make no mistake about it. If you own a small or midsized business, you're going to be flooded with opportunities to get out there and network. In Austin, for instance, you can literally eat every meal during the week at some networking event if you care to do so. Choose wisely.

In theory, I think networking is terrific way to build (or at least lay the foundation for) business relationships. In practice, though, I think it's all too easy to waste a lot of time and money meeting people who don't have the slightest interest in helping you succeed. They're eager enough for any sales leads you can give them — but somehow never find a way to reciprocate. So you tell me: was your time well spent?

Here's an example from my own networking experience. I met a telecommunications consultant who pestered me to attend one of her networking group meetings. She seemed a nice enough person and fairly competent at what she did, so I said yes.

I knew it was a mistake as soon as the meeting started. I was fresh meat to the group members, who took turns gathering around me, pumping my hand, pressing their business cards at me and telling me in painful detail what they did. Nor were they shy about asking me for the names of anyone I thought could use their services. It goes without saying that they weren't particularly interested in what I did.

For some reason, I felt obligated to the woman who had invited me, so I offered to introduce her to a client of mine that I knew was thinking about making changes to his telecom system. No harm, right? I left the event feeling like I'd done a good deed, even if it hadn't been productive from a sales standpoint.

It's all too easy to fall into networking situations where you're expected to treat your contacts like trading cards, swapping them for other prospects.

A few months later, I received a phone call from that same client. But instead of thanking me for having made the connection, he expressed in no uncertain terms his displeasure that I'd ever given his name out. Apparently, this telecommunications consultant had jumped ship to four different companies, and each time she nagged my client with the new company's offerings. He was tired of being bothered, and I was embarrassed that I'd inadvertently been part of it all. No good deed goes unpunished, right?

But the real lesson for me was that your actions can have ripples you don't intend. Network wisely. Network strategically. Network carefully. It's all too easy to fall into situations where you're tempted to (and even expected to) treat your clients and contacts like trading cards, swapping them for other prospects and leads. Don't do it.

Networking expert Lynne Waymon says, "Networking, in

its pure form, enables business people to further their own goals while helping others further theirs. It should be a positive step in the right direction for everyone on the road to success. Networking is a process of building business relationships for the long term."

Negative Networking

The story I just shared with you was a prime example of what I call "Negative Networking." You've probably already had your own experience with Negative Networking, and if not, chances are you will. I know I've seen it more than once, and although the specifics may change, the pattern is always the same.

Meetings tend to be very structured, run with brutal efficiency by a forceful moderator or group leader. Everyone takes turns introducing themselves and their business and saying what leads they're looking for. Group members are strongly encouraged (in some groups, even required) to give out a specific number of leads at each meeting. The emphasis here is on quantity over quality, just in case you had any doubts. The trading card mentality is very much in evidence.

A lot of these groups also discourage you from networking anywhere else or belonging to other networking groups. They want your money, your loyalty and your time, and they accept no excuses.

A friend of mine was once considering joining one of these groups, one that was part of a national franchise. His real sticking point, though, was that the group only permitted three missed lunch meetings per year. For my friend, a small business owner, that was a commitment he was reluctant to make. He explained to the group's coordinator that client obligations, other meetings and project deadlines might interfere with his schedule, and as a lone service provider he didn't have any employees who could fill in for him. Without batting an eye, she told him, "Well, if you can't come, just send one of your clients!" As he told me, "A lot of the value I provide to my clients is that I save them time — and now she wants me to ask them to go to a meeting, not for their own benefit, but to talk about how great I am? Did it ever occur to her that I can't impose on my clients like that? She just doesn't get it."

Needless to say, he didn't join. But plenty of others do, and Negative Networking is becoming an epidemic in the business community. Here are some tips for recognizing Negative Networking in action and ensuring you don't get infected:

1. Negative Networkers talk more about leads than referrals. Referrals, in my opinion, involve a third party willing to link his or her reputation with yours. A referral is calling up a client or contact and saying, "Hey, I know someone whose services would really help your business. He's great. Here's his number." It involves the stamp of approval from someone the prospective client or customers really trusts. Sometimes it even involves the referring person setting up a meeting or going out of his way to ensure that this connection takes place. Referrals are all about trust, value and relationships.

Leads, on the other hand, are simply the names of people or businesses that *might* be interested in your products or services. A person giving you a lead isn't going to help open that door for you — in many cases, because they don't have access themselves. A lead is really just a lottery ticket that says: "Here you go, best of luck, hope it all works out!" As a result, we can waste a lot of time and effort pursuing leads that never materialize into sales.

Any networking group that requires you to churn out the names of friends, family, clients and business associates is leads-focused. Any group that emphasizes sheer numbers over finding the right fit is leads-focused. Any group that expects you to open your rolodex to your fellow members before you get to know them is leads-focused.

2. Negative Networkers value the quick buck over the long-term relationship. In saying this, I don't mean to imply that people in these networking groups are dishonest, incompetent or bad businessmen and women. Many of them are fine, upstanding folks. But they're in an environment that's more focused on immediate gratification — the quick and easy sale — than delivering long-term value. I recently attended one group that almost screamed "Negative Networking" as soon as I walked it. Instead of finding intelligent conversation and a variety of potentially mutually-valuable resources and connections, I was surrounded by money-hungry sales reps on the make for contacts. No one was interested in learning about me and my business or in helping me achieve my goals. I was just a means to an end for them.

3. Negative Networkers talk more than they listen. At these kinds of networking events, the "regulars" will inevitably make the rounds, taking any opportunity to deliver their elevator speech, push a business card at you and let you know exactly what they need and who they're looking for. Hand them a card in return and a surprisingly high number will put it in their pocket without ever looking at it — they're too busy talking. When they've said everything they care to, they'll size up their next victim and move on. Do I even have to mention that these folks aren't the slightest bit interested in what they can do for you?

> **"We talk on principle, but we act on interest."**
>
> — *Walter Savage Landor*

4. Negative Networkers are me-focused. Negative Networkers love to talk about themselves. They love to speculate on potential leads for their companies. They love to brag about their successes. And many of them are very happy to monopolize your time and attention. They'll milk you for advice, ideas and suggestions, but the second the conversation turns to your situation or your goals, they'll find an excuse to move on to their next prospect. I'm sure these are the same folks who, when introduced to a physician at a party, say, "You know, I've been having this sharp, shooting pain right here. What do you think that could be? You wouldn't mind taking a look, would you?"

There's nothing wrong with asking for advice. It's one of the great perks in building a strong network. But Negative Networkers rarely reciprocate. Give them great advice or give them a fantastic referral if you want, but don't expect they'll ever do the same. Worse, many of them aren't even all that appreciative. They're so me-focused that they're oblivious to anything else. I had a friend once give a mutual business acquaintance some terrific marketing advice for a new program. She listened noncommittally. A few months later they saw each other again and she immediately starting gushing about this new idea *she'd* had — the same one he'd given her!

Let me be clear about one thing: some people like this kind of business networking. If it works for you, more power to you. I would never dissuade anyone doing what they think is right for their situation. But what I've found is that any relationships you form through Negative Networking will lack substance. The people you meet don't tend to be the kind to hold any one job for long, and they'll call you only if they need something they think you can provide. Be warned.

Civic Networking

In contrast to Negative Networking, Civic Networking offers much more legitimate opportunities to build mutually-beneficial relationships.

Civic Networking basically brings businesspeople together for some sort of community-oriented purpose. Civic Networking spans everything from the Lions and Rotary Clubs to charitable or even church activities. It enables people with shared values to support a common goal.

Here's my advice about Civic Networking: do it because you believe in the causes these organizations support, not because you think that there might be some sort of short-term business opportunity. While Civic Networking is a terrific way to meet people and build relationships, over-aggressively pursuing business may turn folks off.

In time, those discussions may happen naturally, as you get to know others better and they learn more about you. Just be careful not to force the issue.

Even if your Civic Networking groups never directly result in additional sales, they can still be valuable in expanding your pool of resources. As we saw in Chapter Three, sometimes just knowing someone who knows someone is enough.

Social Networking

Whether it's a business book club or a regular happy hour, Social Networking allows businesspeople to relax and interact more naturally in environments where everyone can let their guard down. Unlike Negative Networking, conversations tend to cover a wider range of topics, and over time you'll probably get a pretty good idea about the personality, character and reliability of your peers. You'll learn not only what they do, but, perhaps more importantly, who they are.

In fact, you can sometimes harvest massive amounts of good information at these events, and many promising introductions (and even deals) have been made over a couple of beers. Just remember why you're there. It's fine to loosen your collar a little, but be careful not to throw your professionalism to the curb. I've seen folks have a few drinks too many and abandon networking for flirting or gossip. That's not the kind of impression you want to leave on people, obviously. I always think of the old saying that loose lips sink ships — some people work these events like they're playing a game of Battleship.

Getting caught up in the socializing itself is unproductive. Time is the most precious commodity you have. Once spent, you can never get it back. So invest it wisely. If you can make one or two promising connections, the event was probably worth your time. But if the only thing you came away with was a beer buzz — well, an evening's fun on your company charge card doesn't change the fact that your odds of success are no better the next day than they were before the event. You've got nothing to show for the time spent — except maybe a hangover!

Strategic Networking

Strategic Networking tries to take some of the hit-and-miss out of the networking experience by bringing together business-people whose services complement each other. The goal is to foster the growth of long-term business alliances rather than quick-'n-dirty sales. Strategic Networking is designed for decision makers rather than sales reps.

These events are often sponsored by Chambers of Commerce, trade or professional organizations, and local business associations. You can find them through your local business journal, through Chamber publications or simply by asking other people what groups or associations they belong to. Tell them that you're looking to expand your "people network." What groups would they suggest you join?

> **"The moment of enlightenment is when a person's dreams of possibilities become images of probabilities."**
>
> — *Vic Braden*

Unlike most Negative Networking groups, these often have some sort of educational component to them. The businesspeople involved want to learn how to become better at what they do and how they do it, and they're also usually eager to help others do the same. There's a spirit of cooperation that's very different from what you'll find at one of those lead-generating lunches.

When I moved to Austin in the early '90s, I felt like I was just this green kid from New Mexico. Although I'd had some success in sales, I soon realized that actually owning a company involved a lot more than just knocking on doors and asking for business. My first dilemma was that I was young, fairly inexperienced and lacked a college degree. None of that bothered me until I began to call on people and regularly hear things like "You're too young to own your own business," or "Seriously, you can't be the guy calling the shots."

It was discouraging. Don't get me wrong, I was used to rejection by this point in my career — but rejection on this level was somehow different. Prospects weren't just saying no; they

were impugning me as a business owner. It's like they were saying that I wasn't worthy of owning a business. That hurt. My self-
confidence began to be shaken, which in turn further negatively
impacted my success. Needless to say, my early days in Austin
were pretty tough ones emotionally .

I decided that I needed to change my strategy. I joined the
Greater Austin Chamber of Commerce, which is an excellent
thing to do if you are new to the city. Even better, I joined one of
the Chamber's pilot programs, something they called Executive
Dialogue. Eleven other business owners and myself met monthly
to discuss business issues, offer suggestions and critique strategy.
It was like having an informal board of directors.

Joining that group was a defining moment in my career
— and my life. I was thrown in with 11 people who were much
better educated and far more experienced. And yet the business
issues they were facing were remarkably similar to the ones I had.
It was liberating to see that despite our varied backgrounds, our
problems were largely the same.

Being part of the Executive Dialogue program gave me confidence, deepened my understanding of the Austin business environment, and gave me a strong core network of business allies. It
also resulted in a number of sales, both for me and for my peers in
the group. To this day, it is still one of the best and most productive examples of strategic networking I've ever experienced.

Network with Purpose

Networking doesn't need to have immediate, dramatic results for it to have been effective. You can't build relationships
with only one meeting, but you can get a good start. There's an
old Chinese saying that says that "even a journey of a thousand
miles begins with a single step."

With that in mind, it's vital you don't make a misstep when
you begin networking. Here are some tips for making the most
out of any event:

1. Determine which networking events to hit and which to

miss. The older I get, the more I value my time. So whenever I evaluate an event, I ask myself a number of questions:

- Will an individual (or individuals) that I want to see be in attendance? If so, will the atmosphere allow us the opportunity to chat with one another?
- Will I learn something new by attending this event?
- Will I meet new people I'd like to know or who I'd like to know me?
- What's the likely return on my investment of time? Can I spend that time more productively somewhere else?

2. Remember why you came. It's not to eat or get drunk or gossip with your buddies. You came to establish mutually beneficial connections with like-minded people. It's fine to have fun, but don't become distracted from your real goals. Before attending an event, it's sometimes useful to make a list of the top three things you want to accomplish there. Writing it down helps make you accountable and keep you on target.

3. Listen, listen . . . and listen some more. You don't have to take a vow of silence, but neither should you monopolize every conversation. And believe me, the more you listen, the greater the chances of establishing a meaningful connection. Remember, you're not just there representing your interests — you're a proxy for all your other business and personal relationships. You might hear something that results in a new opportunity for a friend or colleague, and that karma usually comes back to benefit you, too.

4. Show interest. You can't fake sincerity. There's no greater turn-off than the realization that the person you're talking to has absolutely no interest in anything you're saying. While you're telling them about your business, they're mentally rehearsing their elevator speech or sizing up the rest of the room or thinking about dinner. Tell me, are you going to refer any of your friends, family or clients to that person? Are you going to go out of your way to help them build their business?

Make sure that doesn't happen to you. Take the time to actually look at the business card they hand you before stashing it in your pocket. Make and maintain eye contact. And ask questions: about them, about their business, about their hobbies and interests. You may discover you're both NASCAR fans, or that your wife went to school with his brother. And suddenly . . . bingo! You've made a connection.

> **Networking events offer you a way to make an initial connection. The real business of building a relationship comes afterward.**

5. *Follow up.* Plenty of businesspeople spend countless hours making the networking rounds without anything to show for it because they never take a little extra time to make a follow-up phone call or send an e-mail. Networking events offer you a way to make an initial connection. The real business of building a relationship comes afterward.

Different Strokes for Different Folks

In Chapter Two, we talked a little about the three broad personality categories: Mavens, Relaters and Evangelists. Not surprisingly, each type prefers to network differently. Since you'll encounter all three, here are some tips for what to do (and what not to do) once you've identified which type you're talking to.

Mavens. As a group, Mavens are less proficient at what we usually think of as networking than either Relaters or Evangelists. Being knowledge-driven, they hate small talk, are usually uncomfortable sharing personal information, and are often natural introverts.

That's not to say they don't network. Put a group of Mavens with a shared interest together and they'll gab for hours about all sorts of detailed, complex technical issues. Of course, they're also likely to leave without ever having learned — or cared to learn — each other's names. That's a big networking oops, all right.

Spotting a Maven at a networking function is usually fairly easy. See someone standing apart, not making eye contact and looking like they can't wait to bolt for the door? There's an excellent chance that's a Maven. Start talking to someone and notice that they're keeping a greater than normal distance from you, not making eye contact (again!) and answering only in monosyllables? Probably a Maven. Remember the "low talker" from that episode of *Seinfeld*? Maven.

The key to connecting with Mavens is to make them feel comfortable. Don't crowd them — let them determine their physical proximity to you. If possible, try to subtly maneuver them to the edge of the crowd or a more quiet part of the room. Do what you can to help them feel physically at ease in the environment.

Then slowly draw them out. Ask technically-oriented questions first, then gradually segue into more personal matters. If you can discover a mutual interest, odds are good that they'll open up to you even more quickly.

> **"What we see depends mainly on what we look for."**
>
> — *John Lubbock*

As Bijoy Goswami writes in *The Human Fabric*, "If the topic of conversation is shallow, the Maven has nothing to gain and will disconnect from the conversation. You can always re-engage a Maven by asking his opinion."

Since Mavens are single-taskers as opposed to multi-taskers, conversations with them will often tend to be linear. If you do get a Maven to start waxing eloquently on his or her favorite topic, be careful not to interrupt. Few things will frustrate a Maven more!

Mavens build relationships at their own speed. You can't force it. Concentrate on earning their trust and identifying commonalities. Most Mavens are naturally helpful and effective problem-solvers, so they can be valuable connections to make.

Relaters/Connectors. This is probably the easiest group to network with. They'll make you feel at ease virtually from the moment you meet them, and probably treat you like an old friend from the start. Networking with Relaters is almost as easy as falling off a log, and it's certainly a lot more fun.

Although some Relaters are introverted, the majority of them are very social. They delight in talking, asking questions and discovering mutual connections. As their name suggests, Relaters think in terms of relationships. While you're talking to them, they're busy figuring out exactly where you fit in their relationship web. Do you have any friends in common? Does your neighbor go to their church? Does your wife's cousin live in their hometown? They may not be asking those questions directly, but that's the kind of information they're really seeking. Watch their eyes light up when they find it! As Bijoy writes, "Relaters are more concerned with *context* than *content*."

Trust is very important to Relaters, which is one of the reasons why they'll spend so much time finding out about your background, your family, your friends and your interests. To action-minded Evangelists, in particular, this may seem like they're avoiding getting down to business. In reality, though, they're satisfying themselves that you're someone *worth* doing business with. It's fine to keep them on-track, but resist the impulse to jump ahead too quickly or you might scare them off.

Relaters prefer personal interaction, often with several individuals at a time. They may jump in and out of several simultaneous conversations — unlike Mavens, they are consummate multi-taskers. Again, this can annoy the heck out of linear-thinking Mavens and goal-oriented Evangelists, but that's just the way they are. Interestingly, Relaters may dislike and even avoid "formal" networking events, which often seem too stilted and artificial.

Naturally empathic, Relaters will tend to unconsciously pick up on your subtle emotional and physical cues. It's not at all unusual for them to mirror your posture, energy level and body language. If you notice that, it's a sign they're fully engaged.

Relaters are less likely than the other two groups to offer solutions to problems or concerns you describe. While the Maven says "Here's what you should do," the Relater tends to say, "Here's someone you should talk to." Their impulse is to connect you to potential resources by making you a part of their network.

That's especially true for highly-evolved Relaters. These "Connectors" are continually making . . . well, connections. They're always on the lookout for ways to build mutually-beneficial relationships for all the folks in their network. They see life as a big puzzle, and people are the pieces. Upon meeting you, they're immediately trying to figure out what space you fill.

For Connectors, making the connection is usually a reward in itself. If you want to really make an impression, though, give them access to some of the people in *your* network. What pieces of the puzzle can you make available to them?

Evangelists. Evangelists are all about action. They want to make things happen. They're motivated by causes, quests and goals. Mavens and Relaters see knowledge and relationships (respectively) as ends unto themselves, but for Evangelists they are only means to an end.

On the surface, Evangelists at a networking event don't seem all that dissimilar from Relaters. Both may appear highly social and be surrounded by a group of people. But whereas the Relater acts as the group's facilitator, or perhaps its "host," the Evangelist has to be the center of the group's attention. That's not hard for Evangelists to do, as they naturally exude energy and charisma.

In networking with Evangelists, keep in mind their opportunistic tendencies. Implicit in any conversation with them is the question, "What can you do for me?" If they don't see you as a resource, they'll quickly lose interest and move on to greener pastures. Make yourself useful. Help them see how you, your network, your skill set or your interests benefit their cause.

Evangelists are the most persuasive of the three types and the ones most drawn to controversy. They hold strong opinions about . . . well, virtually everything. And they don't shy away from debate. "Evangelists love nothing more than a good argument," writes Bijoy in *The Human Fabric*. "It's a way of crossing swords and tangling with others, which is an Evangelist's way of getting to know someone." So don't be surprised when the Evangelist you're talking with challenges one of your statements. He's not intentionally being a jerk — he's just taking your measure and, perhaps, having a little fun at your expense. Hold your own and you'll earn his respect.

Most Evangelists would rather talk than listen, so it can sometimes be a challenge getting a word in. Again, the best way to capture their attention is to identify the causes they're passionate about and relate to them. Those causes aren't necessarily political or earth-changing. They might just as easily center on promoting a new kind of marketing, or even a favorite restaurant.

> **Networking can be a powerful tool for building both professional and personal relationships. Or it can be a huge waste of time.**

Because they know how to make things happen, Evangelists are terrific resources. They often have wider, if shallower, networks than Relaters. And by their very nature, they cause ripples — definitely people worth knowing better.

From Networking to Connecting

Networking is only valuable for the ripples it can create. It's up to you to think actively about how to bring these new acquaintances into your relationship network. Who do you know who should know them?

To make a habit about turning networking into connecting, try using the DARE system:

Document. During networking events, listen for key information about a person's likes, dislikes, goals and background. Like a journalist, focus on the "who, what, when, where, why and how." Then write down those bits of information immediately following the event, when they're still fresh in your mind.

Appreciate. Look past the business card to gain an appreciation for an individual *as* an individual. What gifts and talents can they offer the world? Who are they at their core?

Reveal. Don't bury people in your PDA, rolodex or address book. Take proactive steps to reveal these individuals to new people, new associations and new opportunities. Who can they help? Who can help them?

Express. Time is one of the most precious resources we have. Let people know that you appreciate their time and attention, even if it was just a 10-minute conversation at a networking happy hour. Send thank-you cards and e-mails.

Networking can be a powerful tool for building both your business and your personal and professional relationships. Or it can be a huge waste of time. The devil, as they say, is in the details.

For all potential pitfalls, though, I know I'm still an active networker. I still attend networking events to meet new prospects, keep in touch with business acquaintances, and stay current on what's happening in the community. I'm more selective now than I used to be, though, and more disciplined. I know what I have to get from an event for it to be a worthwhile use for my time.

"Real networking," says business author Bob Burg, "is the cultivation of mutually beneficial, give and take, win/win relationships."

I couldn't agree more. Just watch out for those Negative Networkers.

Points to Ponder

- Be careful how you network or you can waste your time, money and opportunities.

- "Negative Networkers" care less about building relationships than swapping leads. They have a trading card mentality towards their clients, contacts, friends and acquaintances.

- There are many kinds of networking opportunities: civic, social and strategic.

- For the best networking results, choose events carefully, remember your purpose for being there, ask questions and listen carefully to the answers, and follow up with any promising connection you make.

- Mavens, Relaters and Evangelists prefer to network differently. Tailor your approach to suit each style: draw Mavens out by asking technical questions, help Relaters place you in their web of connections, and refuse to be intimidated by Evangelists' strong and strident opinions.

Ripple Exercises

- Plan to attend three networking events of some kind this week. Set a goal to meet and meaningfully interact with at least five people at each.

- Find out as much as you can about each person by asking questions and listening to their responses. Identify if each is a Maven, Relater or Evangelist.

- Through follow-up communication and interaction, create positive ripples for at least three of those people within the next 72 hours.

PART 3

Practicing Relationships

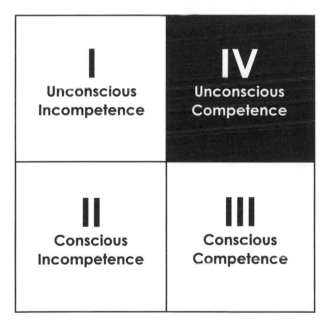

During the summer of 1936, Frederick J. Osius, an amateur inventor and born showman, created what he called a "disintegrating mixer for producing fluent substances." His idea was to sell the invention to restaurants and drugstores as a way of mixing milk shakes and other soda fountain and bar drinks.

Unfortunately, Osius didn't have the money to really develop and market the new contraption. He did, however, have a friend whose brother-in-law was the publicist for Fred Waring, leader of the popular Pennsylvanians band and choral group. Osius used the connection to meet Waring backstage after a Manhattan radio gig. Knowing that Waring was something of a tinkerer himself, Osius tried to demonstrate the prototype in the bandleader's dressing room. The primitive mixer failed to work, but Waring was taken with the concept's potential, both for the market and for himself.

In addition to giving the project a name, the "Waring Blendor," and a significant investment, Waring also connected Osius with Ed Lee, who helped solve some serious mechanical and leakage problems. He was also the Blendor's chief promoter, showing off its capabilities in his dressing room while on tour.

World War II hit the company hard, though, and in 1947 entrepreneur Hazard Reeves offered to take it off Waring's hands. Fascinated by the Blendor's potential, Reeves targeted the home market, and by 1954 over 1,000,000 Blendors had been sold.

And then the really unexpected happened. Hospitals had been early customers, having found the Blendor unsurpassed for preparing baby food. Now laboratories requested specially modified Blendors of their own.

One such machine, renamed the Waring Aseptical Dispersal Blendor, helped Dr. Jonas Salk find a cure for polio. Salk used the Blendor to grind up materials to prepare cultures for his polio vaccine.

And so something invented to make a better milkshake helped cure one of the century's most devastating diseases.

5 | THE ROI OF SELFLESSNESS
Taking relationships to the next level

One of my friends loves to ask, usually after a few beers, "How do you know when a salesman is lying? Easy! His lips are moving!"

Sure, it's not particularly funny, but that's not what caused me to grimace every time I heard him tell the joke. It's the realization that the punchline, in too many cases, hits pretty close to the truth. I saw it time and again during my own sales career, and it always angered and frustrated me.

The fact is, far too many salespeople approach the customer as an adversary instead of an ally. They have a win-lose philosophy, and it doesn't take a lot of imagination to figure out who the loser is. They're only interested in short-term self-gain, and they don't much care what happens to the customer after their check clears.

That's completely wrongheaded, of course, but it's indicative of a profession that often rarely receives any training about the necessity and value of building relationships. And the rest of us suffer as a result.

"What's that got to do with me?" you're asking. "I'm not in sales. I've never been in sales. And, God willing, I'll never, ever be in sales."

Ah, here's the rub. We're all in sales, whether or not we realize it (or want to admit it!). At its heart, successful sales is all about providing solutions and building relationships. Within that context, we're constantly selling ourselves, our ideas, our proj ects and our opinions. Whether we're a Fortune 500 executive or a college grad just entering the job market or a stay-at-home mom, we're all engaged in providing solutions and building relationships.

I was recently asked just what, exactly, sets me apart from my competition. I love it when people ask me that. That question gives me the same thrill baseball players must feel when they see the pitch they expected coming their way and all they have to do is set their hips, take a big swing and send the ball right out of the park.

I think that question — which basically boils down to "Why should I do business with you instead of one of your competitors?" — is so important that asking and answering it should be one of the most important aspects of any sales presentation. Answered correctly, it can give you a degree of credibility none of your competitors can match as well as take a lot of the wind out of *their* presentations.

But it's a question that's relevant even in non-sales situations. For all its seeming simplicity, it really cuts to the heart of who you intend to be as a person and how you go about building relationships and setting positive ripples into motion. "What sets you apart?" is a question that applies equally well to your professional *and* personal life. So I encourage you to ask yourself, "What sets *me* apart?" Are you satisfied with the answer?

The Answer

So what's my answer to that provocative little question? Simple: me. What sets me apart, in life and business, is me. It's not products or services or warranties (although all are very good on anything I'll commit to selling). It's not big houses or fast cars or fat paychecks. It's me — and the relationships I've been able to form, grow and strengthen.

On the face of it, a statement like might seem a little arrogant. But it's not about ego. It's about my commitment to being the best resource I can be for my family, friends, clients and associates. In my business dealings, that means making sure clients know that my goal isn't selling them something — it's to become a trusted part of their team. I want to help them solve problems, pursue opportunities and grow their business. They know I'll be a resource for them, not just some vendor looking for a quick sale and a big check. When they're agonizing over a decision, so am I. When they're overjoyed by the result, so am I.

For me, relationships are always personal. My goal is to serve all my clients as conscientiously and honestly as if they were a friend or family member. If you want to create lasting client trust, I encourage you to do the same. The sooner your clients understand that you see your job not as making a sale, but as acting as a resource for them, the sooner you'll be able to cross the line from vendor to partner.

> "I'm convinced that a lack of consumer trust plagues many salespeople today. It costs companies millions in unrealized sales and profits."
>
> — Ron Willingham

Take the time to understand and empathize with their needs, fears, challenges, opportunities and successes. Be their advocate, their champion and their hero. Celebrate with them in success and help pick them up when times are rough.

Just in case this sounds like professional suicide to you seasoned sales pros out there, let me assure you it's exactly the opposite. Become a valued resource for your clients and the business will come pouring in. Trust me on this — not only have I consistently experienced it in my own business, but I've repeatedly seen it happen for others who adopted a relationship-first strategy.

Just Win, Baby?

Unfortunately, conventional wisdom too often urges us to take a completely different approach: the "Just win, baby!" philosophy of Al Davis, the notorious owner of the Oakland Raiders. And just like Al, who routinely turned a blind eye to players' character faults as long as the victories kept coming, most of the world puts short-term success above everything else. That's true especially in sales, but I've seen it firsthand in virtually every professional and personal context.

But is that how you want to be remembered? Is that how you want to set yourself apart, by sacrificing everything — customer benefit, friendship, even self-respect — for the sake of immediate self-gratification? Is that how you want to define winning — the other guy has to lose?

That's not the world I want to live in. And while I can't wave a magic wand and change human nature or reorder society, I can do my part to create something better for the people I encounter in my life's journey. I can make a difference, one ripple at a time. And so can you.

In life and business, focus on creating win-win situations. Look beyond the immediate sale in order to connect with customers as people. Learn about their companies, their needs and — perhaps most importantly — their goals. Ask yourself, "What can I do now to help them take that next step? How can I help them succeed?" Put your network into action on their behalf, and I think you'll be amazed at the satisfaction you'll feel and the benefits you'll receive. The payoff is truly unbelievable at so many levels.

My relationship resource strategy has been a key factor in helping me achieve business success even during difficult economic times. And although it may sound counterintuitive, often my office equipment business grew because I was a resource in areas other than office equipment. It was when I leveraged my list of business connections or knowledge capital for clients that I became a real partner, a real friend and a real asset. If someone needed information, they knew to call me. Even if I didn't have first-hand knowledge of what they needed, I most likely knew someone who did. And that was a powerful position to be in.

In life and business, focus on creating win-win situations. Look beyond the immediate sale in order to connect with customers as people.

One of my first office equipment customers was a semiconductor company. I went above and beyond the call of duty to get to know one of the key players in the organization and prove my value beyond simply being a reliable vendor. Over the course of several meetings, I learned that her husband was longing to quit his bland corporate job to focus on his true passion — graphic design.

As it happened, another prospect was a local printing company, and I knew that they had recently lost their lead designer. I knew nothing about the job's specific requirements, but it sounded promising, so I made a few calls. Within a few weeks, my semiconductor customer's husband had the job, and both he and his wife were feeling very friendly towards me. And, of course, I suddenly had a very firm foothold for obtaining the printing company's business as well.

If the story ended there, I could feel good about the role I played. But it didn't end there. Several months later, I happened to call my semiconductor friend to touch base. She told me that she had just been told that the company was being moved to California, and that she would be losing her job within a few weeks. She was understandably upset.

Again I started making calls. By the end of the following week, I had helped her find another job with a prospect I'd been calling on for months. I don't know whether that company's owner felt guilty that he hadn't yet committed to me, or if he simply recognized a good thing when he saw it, but the result was a win-win for both his company and my friend.

Since then, my friend has worked for two more companies, and in each position she has utilized my company to fulfill their office equipment needs. She's also referred at least three other companies to me that became clients. If you calculate the strict monetary "value" of that relationship, it's provided almost $150,000 in direct and indirect revenue to my business. And it's all because I decided to become a resource for her instead of treating her as a walking dollar sign!

The ROI of Selflessness

I recently heard an anonymous saying that I really liked: "The most selfish thing a person can do is be selfless." As I thought about it, I decided it was even more accurate to say: "The most *self-serving* thing a person can do is be selfless." I've discovered that in selflessly helping others, you're really serving yourself. It may not happen today or next week or even next year, but trust me: it will happen. Somehow, somewhere, in some way, your relationship investment will pay dividends — sometimes huge ones.

Human nature being what it is, it often takes an act of will to act selflessly. We're constantly being advised to mind our own business, look the other way and not involve ourselves in something that doesn't directly concern us. But the power of the ripple effect is that it's often the indirect influences that impact us most. So don't listen to the so-called "conventional wisdom." One of the best things you can do for both your professional and personal life is to reach out to others. Whether it's the mom on your son's tee-ball team who is looking to reenter the work force or a guy at the bar who wants to change jobs, pay attention to their needs and try to help them if possible.

Whether or not you see direct, tangible or immediate benefits from your selflessness, at the very least you've just added value to your relationship with another person.

It's important when approaching these situations not to expect anything in return. If you're playing some angle, odds are that person will sense it and become wary, maybe even resentful. Help someone get a leg up in life and I guarantee that the good you do will be returned to you in one form or another. But remember, whether or not you see direct, tangible or immediate benefits from your selflessness, at the very least you've just added value to your relationship with another person. As that relationship becomes stronger, the ripples it generates may well help you in other areas.

The comic author Leo Rosten once wrote, "The secret of acting is sincerity. Once you have learned to fake that, you are made." Trust me — don't try to fake it. If you do, you'll likely sabotage your relationship. Either develop a sincere interest in helping others better their lives and careers, or stay away. The moral middle ground is really just a no-man's-land.

Taking action without first calculating about how the result might impact you personally is a tough habit to break. We've been conditioned to be a "me-first" generation focused primarily on our own needs, fears and desires. But if you can break that habit and form a new one, one that embraces selfless thinking, your life will be enriched beyond your wildest imagination. Trust me on this.

For those of you who are already charitably-minded, adopting a selfless attitude in the workplace probably won't be that difficult. In all likelihood, you'll just need to make a little more of a conscious effort than you have in the past. But the underlying motivations (and even habits) are probably already there. Take them out, dust them off, and begin putting them into more frequent and regular practice.

For the rest of us, it's a little tougher. Take me, for instance. Although I had three brothers and sisters, I was the youngest by 10 years — an unexpected surprise, my parents later said. Given the age difference, I grew up with more of an only-child mindset. I was a little spoiled, and more than a little self-centered. What interactions I did have with my siblings seemed to center around me protecting *my* toys, *my* space and *my* stuff. I guess I developed some of the worst symptoms of only-child syndrome and mixed it with a dose of sibling rivalry.

As an adult, I began to see how much I'd internalized those childhood habits and behaviors. Not to put too fine a point on it, I became selfish. Heck, I still am (that'll make my wife smile!). I'm still very . . . protective of the things I own and hold dear, and my natural tendency is to still think of myself first.

I was fortunate, though, to experience a kind of epiphany about just how much that attitude was limiting my life and the lives of the people around me. I realized that I had to make a change, and that by beginning to selflessly help others, I was ultimately helping myself: "The most *self-serving* thing a person can do is be selfless." I get it now, and not only is my life better for it, but so are the lives of my family, friends, employees and clients.

Building Trust

Obviously, it takes more than a selfless attitude and a resource-oriented approach to create the kind of relationships I've talked about in this book. It also takes time, commitment and perseverance through both good times and bad. Think about your close friends. I'm betting that the ones in your inner circle are the ones who have been through the fire with you, the ones who have seen you and supported you when you were weak or sad or in pain, the ones for whom you've done likewise. Without those traumatic but defining moments, would your relationships with them be as strong?

Relationships have layers. I'm sure you've seen geologic models of the earth, the ones that show how, if you peeled the planet like an onion, you'd encounter first the crust, then the mantle, then the outer and inner cores. I think that's a simple but effective way of thinking about relationships as well. How many of the relationships in your life never break the surface? How many really reach a person's emotional core?

The relationships in your life are your greatest source of strength, success and fulfillment. Take them seriously. Treat them with the respect they deserve, or risk making some catastrophic mistakes.

I recently took a personal inventory and found that, despite having a tremendous number of relationships with a wide variety of people, I had very few "core" relationships. I suspect that that's the case with most people. But it got me wondering. Why did I have such deep, trusting relationships with certain people and not others? What common features did those relationships possess?

I decided to map my relationships with friends, family, clients, co-workers and business associates. In doing so, I hoped to better understand relationship building in general — why some relationships grow, why some stagnate, and why some dissolve entirely. The result, although based on a lot of interviews, reading and personal reflection, is entirely unscientific. But I've found the Depth of Relationship Model a useful guide in discovering where individual relationships stand.

DEPTH OF RELATIONSHIP MODEL

By identifying a relationship's current level, we're in a better position to work to strengthen it. Not every casual contact is going to result in a lifelong bond, obviously, but I'm betting that there are more than a few relationships with untapped potential in your life, just like there are in mine. By identifying those, we can become more intentional about how we develop them.

And remember, this is more than idle curiosity. The relationships in your life are your greatest source of strength, success and fulfillment. Take them seriously. Treat them with the respect they deserve, or risk making some catastrophic mistakes.

Take John and Teresa, for example. Having met in college, they dated exclusively for almost five years before bowing to pressure from family and friends to get married. On paper, it seemed a good match. They had common interests, had fun together and genuinely cared for each other. But storm clouds appeared not long after the wedding.

The first squall was over John's regular Friday night poker game with the guys. It hadn't seemed an issue while he and Teresa were dating, but now she began to increasingly resent being left home alone. That he usually came back drunk and penniless did little to improve her mood. Nor did the fact that his Saturday mornings and afternoons were often spent "recovering" on the couch from the previous night's party.

"To carry a grudge is like being stung to death by one bee."

— *William H. Walton*

Teresa retaliated by spending more time with friends after work — and spending more of the couple's funds shopping. As the distance between the two grew, so did their credit card bills. John, meanwhile, began spending his evenings out with the guys since he hated the thought of sitting home alone. Often he returned home long after his wife had gone to bed.

Gradually their mutual resentment became mistrust and, finally, outright hostility. Not surprisingly, their young marriage ended in divorce.

So what happened? How could this couple have proved so incompatible, so soon into their marriage? Were there hints earlier in their relationship, warning signs that they (and their friends and family) ignored?

In hindsight, it's evident (to me, at least) that despite having dated for five years, John and Teresa never really understood each other's values, priorities and tendencies. The seeds of mistrust were sown before, not after, their marriage. Were they really ready for the kind of commitment they were making? Obviously not.

Nor are they a unique case. Many of the divorced friends and associates I interviewed reported similar situations. Several told me that they didn't see the "real" person until after they were married, when behaviors or habits or secrets "suddenly" appeared.

Maybe it seemed sudden to them, but I'm betting the clues were already there. If they'd only been able to take a step back and realize that their relationship wasn't as deep as their hormones led them to believe. I know, I know — easier said than done, right?

But if our romantic relationships all too often defy our attempts at objectivity, our social and business relationships are easier to map. Before you can move forward — with a friend, a prospective business partner or even a casual coffee shop acquaintance — you have to know where you are.

Using the Depth of Relationship Model

Read the descriptions below and think about where your relationships fall on the chart on page 99.

Level 1: Awareness

Awareness is a general, surface-level awareness of a person. Maybe you've seen them regularly at a restaurant you frequent, or pass the time of day at the grocery store. You probably know one or two facts about who they are or what they do, but not much more. The two of you aren't exactly strangers, but you could never be classified as friends. You just don't know each other well enough.

For instance, I met a man who owns a carpet cleaning company at a recent networking event. I'm aware of who he is and what he does, but I know nothing about him personally. I don't know how he treats his customers or what his business ethics are like. Would I consider loaning him my car? Not at this stage of the relationship.

Awareness is the starting point for every relationship. Before you can get to know someone, you first have to know *of* them.

Level 2: Rapport

I define rapport as a satisfying relationship with another person that involves a basic level of communication and mutual support. Sometimes we think of rapport as a kind of initial good "chemistry." We might enjoy talking to each other, for example, but at this stage it's still strictly an arm's length relationship. Good rapport with a professional associate might mean you're comfortable doing business with them at some level but you wouldn't ask them to watch your kids.

Building rapport with someone allows for a more direct understanding of the person, what they do and for what, on a very basic level, you can count on them. You want to make a positive impression on them and avoid revealing anything that might harm their perception of you.

Rapport is the most preliminary level of trust. Before a relationship can advance, it's absolutely imperative that rapport exist. But keep in mind that most relationships, especially business relationships, don't advance much beyond the rapport stage, if at all. If you want to grow a relationship, it will likely take some work from here on out.

Level 3: Security

At this stage, you feel less vulnerable in a relationship. You're confident they'll keep their word and deliver on their promises, and that they're not looking to exploit you. As a result, you instinctively lower some of your defenses, both venturing more honest opinions of your own and listening to more of theirs.

You might have reached this level with a neighbor, especially one you wouldn't hesitate to leave your house key with while you're on vacation. Perhaps it's a co-worker you're comfortable enough with to accept their help on a project that's running behind — you know they would never try to corner the credit or make you look bad in front of the boss, and you trust their ability. They've "got your back" during times of pressure or stress, and you've got theirs.

Level 4: Ancillary Trust

Ancillary means "additional," and that's exactly what ancillary trust is — an additional layer of trust. Though neither of you is likely to divulge all of your deep dark secrets to each other, you are more open about your flaws. You'll go out of your way to help this person if possible and unconsciously will be on the lookout for anything that might benefit them.

Strong relationships develop at this stage. You understand what the relationship means to each other, and there is a great deal of compatibility and strong mutual respect. People whose relationship has reached this stage will help each other, even at significant personal, professional or financial risk. They'll run those risks because they have absolute confidence that the other person won't let them down.

> **"Friendship is the only cement that will ever hold the world together."**
>
> *— Woodrow Wilson*

Reaching this layer of ancillary trust may take years, and probably only happens with a relatively small number of people in your life. As with any good building, laying a good foundation can't be rushed. The same is true for a really solid and rewarding relationship.

Level 5: Inner Level of Trust

By now you're probably thinking, "How many layers of trust are there, anyway? Is it really that difficult to trust someone?" But think about it like this: so often our lives are built on pretense. We project an image of ourself to the world at large — not a false image, exactly, but an incomplete one. We refrain from hanging our dirty laundry out in public if possible.

Once you've reached the inner level of trust with someone, all those dark secrets are exposed. And that's OK. You know the other person isn't going to judge you or hate you or reveal them to the world. You can confide in each other with confidence. You know that you'll support each other unstintingly, unwaveringly and fully. It's a great feeling.

The relationships that reach this level are likely to become lifelong friendships. There won't be many of them, but they will be rich and deeply rewarding.

Level 6: Bond

Few of us have the privilege of experiencing a true bond — the culmination of a very special relationship advancing as far as it possibly can. All the mysteries, reservations and defenses of the earlier levels dissolve. You feel like you know this person as well as you know yourself, and you've developed such a strong connection that nothing, good or bad, can tear this down.

This level extends well beyond trust. You'd literally give up your life for the other person, that's how much they mean to you. I believe many, if not most, parents form this bond at the birth of their children (although it may not, sadly, be reciprocated) and it lasts a lifetime, no matter what they do as they grow up. They become the center of your universe. You hurt when they hurt and you rejoice in their good fortune and success.

I also believe most marriages that end in divorce do so because the spouses fail to achieve this critical bond. I describe this stage by borrowing a line from one of my favorite movies, *Jerry McGuire*: "You complete me." For me, that captures the essence of the relationship bond, a bond I believe is critical to successfully making a lifelong commitment.

Bonds occur most often between husbands and wives and parents and children, but they aren't limited to the family unit. Lifelong best friends can reach this level. In fact, given the proper patience and nourishment, people that just plain connect can eventually form a bond.

Taking It to the Next Level

Very few relationships ever reach the bond stage, and that's OK. You can still have many mutually satisfying and beneficial relationships at other levels. The important thing is to identify where your relationships are and where you'd like them to be, and then create a strategy for getting there.

Developing and deepening the relationships in your life doesn't have to involve earth-shaking events. More often that maturation process is the cumulative effect of a lot of little things — a pattern of conscientiousness and selflessness.

To break your old self-centered habits and create new selfless ones, here are a few exercises for you to do. They certainly helped me begin seeing the universe from a different vantage point — one that didn't center on me. In taking these small steps, I ventured for the first time in my life out into a wider, more beautiful and exciting world. My relationships grew (both in quantity and quality) and both I and the people around me became happier.

Step 1: Consciously help at least one person today. Whether it's opening a door, carrying groceries or helping finish a report, these basic, courteous behaviors (which so many of us have learned to ignore) are the building blocks of selfless behavior. Start small, build big.

Step 2: Come in early or stay late at work at least three times next week. Your goal isn't just getting a leg up on your own tasks, but to contribute at some level to the overall work environment. Maybe it's reorganizing your office, or cleaning a common area, or helping out on a project that needs some extra care and attention. It's amazing to see how your perspective changes when you use "your time" to help achieve something that isn't directly yours.

Step 3: Compliment at least one person who is important to you every day. Take the time to praise your spouse, your child, your co-worker or your employee. It's amazing what an impact these spontaneous compliments can have on someone. And they don't have to be lavish. I once had a receptionist who absolutely refused to be proactive or pitch in on projects outside of her direct area of responsibility, no matter how often I asked. Eventually, I decided to try a different tack. I began complimenting her on her outfits and on what a positive, professional impression she made on our customers. Before long, she was eagerly looking for ways to help — without being asked! Once she felt more appreciated, she wanted to reciprocate.

It's never too soon to begin strengthening the relationships in your life. Don't wait until the New Year, or until after that next big project is finished, or until you land that one juicy account.

Do it now. The sooner you begin, the sooner you'll see the results reflected in the people around you. Once you start living your life for others as much as for yourself, I think you'll be amazed at the results.

Points to Ponder

- Whether you're in sales or not, relationships are critical for professional success.

- Look for win-win business scenarios. Consciously become advocates and champions for clients and co-workers.

- The most selfish thing a person can ever do is be selfless.

- Relationships have progressively deepening layers: awareness, rapport, security, ancillary trust, inner level of trust and bond. The deeper a relationship, the stronger it is.

- It is possible to consciously deepen relationships.

Ripple Exercises

- Using the Depth of Relationship Model, chart three personal and three professional relationships. Where are they? Identify specific actions you can take to help create a deeper relationship with those people.

- Consciously help at least one person today.

- Plan to arrive at work early or stay late at least three times next week. Use the extra time to help a colleague or employee.

- Compliment at least one person important to you every day this week.

During the late middle ages, silk was all the rage among European aristocrats. A major problem that confronted weavers, though, was that silk threads were much finer than wool or linen, and the looms of the day had trouble handling such a delicate material. As fashions became increasingly complex, the silk weavers were desperate to find a more economical solution.

The answer came in 1725 from Basile Bouchon, the son of an organ maker who punched different patterns of holes in a role of paper fitted around a pair of cylinders. As the paper moved, horizontal rods attached to wires controlling the loom's threading mechanism moved in and out of the holes, allowing for varying designs. The basic principle was derived from the inner workings of the organs his father made.

A couple of decades later, Jacques de Vaucanson refined the model by punching the holes directly in a cylinder and then wrapping the patterned paper around it. His automatic loom worked so well that the silk weavers of Lyon rioted over what they saw as a threat to their livelihood. Vaucanson's loom was discarded for half a century, stored in pieces in the Paris Museum of Arts and Crafts.

In 1800, a silk weaver named Joseph Marie Jacquard put it back together, with one major modification: he replaced the paper with belt-mounted cards, each carrying a separate section of the pattern.

Before the 1890 U.S. census, an army doctor named John Shaw Billings got the idea of using Jacquard's cards to automate the counting and data filing. He suggested as much to a young engineer, Herman Hollerith, who took the idea and ran with it. Hollerith used dollar-bill-sized cards and punched holes in predetermined positions relating to the type of data recorded.

Hollerith's "tabulator" worked superbly, and within a few years was being used in adding machines and calculators. Years later, the concept became the foundation for the binary "yes-no" code that governs the operation of the computers that run our modern world.

6 | RELATIONSHIP TOOL BOX

*Relationship-building techniques
for life and business*

In the 1987 blockbuster *Wall Street*, unscrupulous tycoon Gordon Gecko (played by Michael Douglas) reveals one of the secrets of his success: "The most valuable commodity I know is information." While I would never pattern either my business or personal dealings on Gecko's example, I can't disagree with him on this point. Information is vital for business success at any level.

With the coming-of-age of the Internet in the 1990s, it's never been easier to harvest massive amounts of information. Perhaps predictably, though, quantity doesn't equal quality. What's really reliable and accurate? And what's only rumor, speculation and outright falsehood?

The fact is, we need good information more than ever — and more of us than ever are prepared to pay for it. Consider Austin-based Hoover's, Inc., one of the net's preeminent sites for searchable business information. During the dot-com gold rush, Hoover's offered most of its services free of charge, depending instead on revenue from site advertisers. But after the crash, the company brass re-evaluated their business model and came to the conclusion that charging a subscription fee to users was a better option.

Turns out they were right. Today the company offers a variety of subscription levels that provide access to proprietary information about 40,000 companies, more than 300,000 corporate officers and 600 industries. Users can create customized searches, download data into spreadsheets and other software, and receive personalized news alerts. A staff of over 80 professional editors collects, evaluates and filters the information to ensure its accuracy and timeliness.

I bet old Gordon G. wishes he'd had access to *that*.

The Relationship Economy

Good information is like money. It's so valuable precisely because it's scarce. It's the same reason why corner offices will always be more prestigious than interior ones — everyone wants one, and there simply aren't enough to go around. Information is like currency in another way, too. Unless you actually *do* something with it, it's not really worth anything. Money is valuable not for what it is (slips of paper), but for what it can get us: food, shelter, clothing, box seats at Texas Stadium.

I often hear talk about the "information economy." But for that information to have any real value, it really depends on a more fundamental "relationship economy" for its transmission. Without that relationship economy, none of us could acquire new customers, vendors or employees. None of us could develop new products or services. None of us could take advantage of new trends and new technologies. Without that relationship economy, there wouldn't *be* any new trends or technologies!

The implications of the relationship economy/information economy interchange are enormous, but for the time being I want to focus on three main lessons. One, all of us are in the relationship-building business. Two, all of us should constantly be on the lookout to gather new information and acquire new knowledge. Three, it's vital that we then disseminate that knowledge through our network of connections, acquaintances, clients, customers, friends, colleagues and family. Only then does information become the dynamic social currency it should be.

Let's look at each of those three points in a little more detail:

1. All of us are in the relationship-building business. If you've been in business for longer than 30 minutes, I'm sure you've heard the old adage, "People do business with people they like and trust." It's true! That's the essence of good customer service, which inspires both customer loyalty and quality referrals.

People also want to help the people they like and trust . . . and know. Mark, a client of mine who also became a good friend, was someone I desperately wanted to introduce to a wider circle of my friends and business associates. I kept looking for ways to add value to his company and our relationship, but for years I was unsuccessful. His business was highly specialized, and somehow the opportunities I wanted to help him develop never quite clicked.

And then over one particular lunch I learned that Mark was an avid scuba diver. It wasn't the kind

> **"Find ways to move your relationships with clients to a level of mutual assistance that goes beyond the core product or service that brought you together in the first place."**
>
> — *Bill Cates*

of information that tends to come up during the normal course of business — and that's precisely what made it valuable. Later on in that conversation, Mark mentioned the frustration he was experiencing with a programmer he had contracted to develop a database program. Despite having spent a lot of money, the project still hadn't gotten off the ground.

And suddenly . . . a connection! I thought of another friend, Eric, who, as luck would have it, was both a superb programmer and a diving enthusiast. I made a call, got the two together and watched them both benefit.

2. All of us should constantly be on the lookout to gather new information and acquire new knowledge. We acquire knowledge through both active and passive means. The Internet, for all its imperfections, is an invaluable tool for actively seeking information. The news we used to get solely from a morning newspaper or an evening telecast can now be accessed within seconds any time we want it. Want to find out who's living in your subdivision? What businesses have just relocated to your city? Consumer spending trends? The web is generally your first stop. It shouldn't be your only stop, though. Books, magazines and newspapers are all worth at least scanning regularly.

Sometimes, though, the most useful bits of knowledge are discovered accidentally. I've found that the simple art of listening is the best way to passively absorb mountains of information. But how many of us take the time to really listen to what's going on around us? Too much of the time, we're talking ourselves! And if we're not, we're thinking about what we're *going* to say, or what we have left to do that day, or what traffic is going to be like on the way home.

> **"Very few men are wise by their own counsel, or learned by their own teaching. For he that was only taught by himself had a fool for his master."**
>
> — *Ben Johnson*

How many valuable pieces of knowledge have we ignored in our lives by being preoccupied with something other than what's being said? What if even one of those pieces could have transformed our lives for the better? What an unrecognized tragedy.

So close your mouth and open your ears! Listen — really listen — when people talk about their interests, their work, their concerns and their hopes. Listen to the Oprahs and Donalds of the world as well as to the waitress who serves you your coffee or the barber who cuts your hair. You never know from which mouth pearls of wisdom will drop.

3. It's vital that we then disseminate that knowledge through our network of connections, acquaintances, clients, customers, friends, colleagues and family. I firmly believe that information is meant to be used, and I'm constantly looking for opportunities to use it wisely and well to create positive ripples. I encourage you to do the same; I think you'll be amazed at the results.

I had a client with whom I wanted to create a closer working relationship. I knew my services could also benefit his client base, and I wanted the chance to forge a connection with some of them. Although my client and I had become fairly good friends, he wasn't sending me a lot of referrals. It wasn't because he was in any way unhappy with the service I was giving him. Like most of us, he simply hadn't embraced a referral-focused, relationship-oriented mindset.

So over the course of several months, I began actively looking for information I knew both he and his clients would find interesting, valuable and educational. I forwarded him links to various websites. I clipped articles and sent them to him with a little note: "I ran across this and thought of you and your clients." I never attached any strings or set any expectation of what I wanted in return. Each time, though, he thanked me with an e-mail, a phone call, a handwritten note or even, on occasion, lunch.

Thanks to those simple actions, our relationship grew stronger and he did even more business with my company — in and of itself something that more than justified my efforts. But one day he all but demanded that I tell him some way he could return the favor. After all, he said, his firm had materially benefited from the additional value I'd helped him create for his clients. He wanted to repay me with something more than lunch, and he wouldn't take "No" for an answer.

So I told him: introduce me to a couple of the clients my "knowledge gathering" had helped. He did even better, and before long seven of his top-shelf clients were also clients of mine. What a return on my minimal investment of time and thoughtfulness!

People Power

Good companies innately understand that commerce revolves around people both internal and external to the business. We talk about "managing" relationships with customers, with vendors and with employees, but I think that's the wrong terminology. Companies grow not by managing those relationships, but by nourishing them.

It's a difference in philosophy. Managing is reactive. It involves adapting to changing circumstances, dealing with conflict and crisis, and, in general, making the best of less than ideal situations. There's nothing wrong with that, but I think it's akin to treading water. You're keeping afloat, but you're not going anywhere. And sooner or later, fatigue is going to send you under for good.

Nourishing, in contrast, is proactive. It results in growth, and it helps create a better, stronger organism. It also often results in a positive return. Nourish your vegetable garden and enjoy the freshest salads on the block. It's satisfying for both the one giving and the one receiving nourishment, what scientists call a "positive symbiotic relationship." Simply put, both parties benefit from the relationship.

What's the business value of nourishing key relationships with customers, vendors and employees? Let's find out.

1. Customers, clients and prospects. This is probably the area where the power of relationships has the most visible impact on a company's bottom line. It bears repeating: "People do business with people they like and trust." A good working relationship with a prospect or current customer often means the difference between making a sale or not, *regardless of the merits of the product or service being offered.* That's not an excuse to sell shoddy merchandise — it's the reality that sales are more influenced by relationships than fancy features.

Your relationship with the client also extends far beyond the immediate transaction. It may significantly impact your long-term profitability. Superior companies not only understand that, they embrace it. They're not just concerned about today's sale; they're intent on maximizing the customer's "lifetime value."

What constitutes lifetime value? It's everything a particular client or customer will spend for the next 10 years or more with your company . But that's not all. It's also all the people your happy, satisfied customer refers to you, and all the money they spend, and all the people they in turn refer and the money *they* spend, and . . . well, you get the idea. Needless to say, a customer's lifetime value can be absolutely tremendous.

To really maximize lifetime value, treat every client opportunity as if you were helping your 90-year-old grandmother. Take the time to look in on your clients, watch out for them and treat them with the respect they deserve. Go the extra mile for them; add value wherever and whenever you can. If you make them feel like a million bucks whenever they interact with you, you can be confident that they'll keep coming back.

2. *Vendors and suppliers.* Too many companies neglect these very important relationships. Big mistake! Without their support and the positive ripples they generate for us, most of us can't deliver our goods and services on time and on budget to our customers. To make its cars, Ford Motor Company needs the assistance of plenty of other businesses: steel, tires, glass, plastics and electronics, just to name a few. For McDonalds to offer that 99-cent cheeseburger, they need relationships with beef distributors (who in turn depend on cattle ranchers), vegetable producers, bread makers and packaging companies.

> **"Fair play with others is primarily not blaming them for anything that is wrong with us."**
>
> — *Eric Hoffer*

It's not that companies don't recognize the important role their suppliers play. I think that all too often they simply see their vendors as necessary evils instead of as partners in a common cause. That's unfortunate, because strong relationships at this level can produce some tremendous benefits.

For example, who do you think gets the first crack at special pricing, better turnaround times and more flexible (and therefore more profitable) terms — the companies a vendor actually likes working with, or the ones who constantly nitpick, delay payment and make unreasonable demands? The answer is obvious.

I think of one vendor in particular, a leasing company that I worked with when I owned an office equipment company. Through them I was able to purchase for resale equipment that had either been repossessed or returned at the lease's expiration. I worked hard to nourish my relationship with the company and became friends with several of the leasing agents. I never missed a chance to thank them for their help and often sent them flowers, notes and cookies.

The result? I usually had the first option to buy topflight equipment, sometimes for mere pennies on the dollar. That translated into much higher margins on my resale opportunities, which significantly helped our profits. Compare that to another office products dealer I knew who lacked that same special relationship with the leasing company. He was paying full price for *his* end-of-lease acquisitions. Ouch.

Finally, I asked my friends at the leasing company why they gave me special treatment. "We like you, Steve," they told me. "You're a valued partner with us, and we go the extra mile for our partners."

3. Employees and co-workers. I recently completed a consulting engagement with a client company that was facing a severe personnel crisis. Employee turnover was high, morale was low, and constructive communication between the owner and his staff was practically nonexistent. And things were only getting worse.

Surprisingly, this wasn't a bad company by any means. The owner had built it from the ground up through hard work and a personal dedication to client service. It had enjoyed success relatively early and had expanded rapidly within the past few years.

> **"If we are facing in the right direction, all we have to do is keep on walking."**
>
> — *Ancient Buddhist proverb*

That, I suspected, was part of the problem. The owner was so focused on his external relationships with clients that he was simply unprepared to nourish his company's internal relationships. Although he had hired talented people, he had provided little training and support and was impatient with their not-unexpected growing pains. His criticism stung more often than not, and his tendency when faced with questions or results not up to his exacting standards was usually to tell the offending employee, "Forget it — just let me do it." In short, the guy was a control freak.

I've found that that's not unusual in entrepreneurs who have bootstrapped their way to success. Sad to say, I think that's a fair characterization of myself when I started my first company. If anything, I was probably an even worse office tyrant than this man. Left uncorrected, it is behavior that can severely limit a business's long-term stability and growth potential.

Companies are no less dependent on their employees than on their vendors to deliver quality service. McDonalds needs its food suppliers, its packagers *and* the folks who take your order (and your money) at the drive-thru. It's *people* who flip the burgers, change the oil in the fryer and pour the shakes. It's *people* who interact with the customers. Even in a company like McDonald's, where management has spent millions to create as automated and system-driven an environment as possible, it's still the front-line

> In a workplace infected by suspicion, fear, mistrust, frustration and animosity, service suffers. Productivity suffers. Customer service suffers. And, ultimately, profitability suffers.

employee who most directly impacts the customer experience. People — not machines, processes or models — are the pathway by which money flows from customers to companies.

And ultimately how employees treat customers is directly dependent on how they are treated by co-workers, supervisors and managers. If they feel valued, respected and rewarded, they will unconsciously transmit that positive energy to all customer interactions. They will be more efficient and innovative, work harder, and be less likely to jump ship to another company. Their talents and skills will be maximized.

The reverse is also true. In a workplace infected by suspicion, fear, mistrust, frustration and animosity, service suffers. Productivity suffers. Customer service suffers. And, ultimately, profitability suffers.

That was the downward spiral my client was likely to enter if things didn't change soon. Fortunately, there was still time to reverse the negative trends. The problem, as I told the frustrated staff, wasn't that their boss didn't want them or the company to succeed. It was that he was scared: scared to lose clients, scared to delegate the work he had done for so long, scared to trust others to care about the company as much as he did.

So I challenged the staff to put themselves in their employer's shoes and work as though they owned the business. I asked them to function with the same energy and sense of urgency he did, and to imagine that they were personally responsible for writing those big payroll checks twice a month.

For the next two weeks, the staff ran like the wind. Customer calls had never been so quickly and efficiently resolved, and new accounts had never been so smoothly and promptly handled. Their energy overwhelmed the control freak owner. By the time he had gotten around to addressing tasks outside his area of core responsibility, they were already correctly completed.

As a result, he was basically forced to learn to trust his employees. And they, in turn, gained an appreciation for the pressures and responsibilities he daily felt. Armed with this new mutual understanding and respect, the entire company began to function in greater harmony.

Creating "Top of Mind" Relationships

Good business depends on good relationships. Simple enough, right? It probably would be, if life itself wasn't so darn complex. But nurturing relationships, whether with customers, vendors or employees, takes time and effort. Too often, we don't feel we have enough of either to give. We get so mired in the details of everyday life that we're just trying to get through the day. That reactive, treading-water mindset that characterizes shortsighted management technique too often affects our relationship building as well.

It's natural, but it's not good. Relationships left on cruise control eventually lose energy and direction. Think about the Relationship Depth Model in Chapter Five. Have some of the relationships in your life become shallower? What were some of the reasons? If you're like most of us, lack of contact is one of the major ones.

There's a lot of talk these days about a marketing concept called "top of mind" awareness. Our brains catalog and store huge amounts of information. But what's on your mental speed dial? What images jump to mind if I mention fast food restaurants? Current movies? Department stores?

Companies desperately want to be the first name on that list, and they annually spend billions of advertising dollars hoping to elevate themselves to the top of your mental awareness.

> **Customers aren't loyal to commercials, but rather to the companies (and, more precisely, the people in those companies) that have consistently delivered value.**

Top of mind awareness depends on contact. Advertising contact, though, is impersonal. It can create brand awareness, but it can't build relationships. Customers aren't loyal to commercials, but rather to the companies (and, more precisely, the people in those companies) that have consistently delivered value. If we want the best kind of top of mind awareness, we've got to stay in touch with the people our business depends on. Because if it's not our name at the head of their mental list when a need arises or an opportunity presents itself, it's obviously going to be someone else's.

In an ideal world, we'd all have the time, energy and resources to personally and frequently contact all those customers, vendors and employees. Since our hectic world is anything but ideal, we need a strategy to help us build those relationships using what we do have: limited time, limited resources and limited room for error.

There are any number of talented, successful businesspeople I could undoubtedly tap for insights in this area. But one of the best frameworks I've found comes from an unlikely source: former UCLA basketball coach John Wooden. Wooden coached the Bruins from 1948 to 1975, leading them to 10 national championships (including an unequalled seven consecutive ones), four perfect seasons and 38 straight NCAA tournament victories. The most successful coach in the history of college basketball, he was elected to the Hall of Fame both as a player and a coach.

Coach Wooden's success was the result of arduous preparation. He stressed practice, teamwork and the fundamentals. Interestingly, he didn't win his first national title until his 15th season at UCLA, but it's pretty clear from what followed that he had spent the time building a system geared for sustainable success.

In an interview with motivational guru Tony Robbins, Wooden laid out the four pillars of his success: planning, practicing, executing and reviewing. These principles, I believe, are the same ones that govern a successful relationship-building strategy.

Plan Wisely

Ever been on a poorly-planned camping trip? One where someone forgot to bring a can opener or the matches or the tent stakes? Wasn't a lot of fun, was it? Relationship building is no different. Leave it to chance and, sooner or later, you'll regret it. As much as we all want to just jump in and "do it," without a sound plan, we're really asking for trouble.

Coach Wooden attributed much of his success to his almost-fanatical planning regimen. Before any practice, he spent a minimum of two hours mapping out precisely what he wanted to accomplish during the practice. He committed all his thoughts and objectives to paper in a very detailed fashion — and he did it every day!

Most of us probably shudder at the idea. A lot of us action-oriented types chafe at planning and tend to see it as time we could better spend "really doing something." But planning *is* doing something! It's laying the groundwork for success. It's not a waste of time, or even a necessary evil, but rather an investment that will pay a huge return.

Consider NASA's Apollo program of the 1960s. President Kennedy announced his vision of landing men on the moon (and bringing them safely home) in 1961. But not until October 1968 did the first manned Apollo flight leave the launchpad. And not until July of the following year did Apollo 11 touch down on the lunar surface. Hundreds of thousands of people were involved in the Apollo program, its budget was essentially unlimited, and still it took over seven years before astronauts ever actually rode the rockets!

But consider more closely what happened. NASA and its contractors spent seven years planning, testing, modifying and planning some more before the first manned Apollo flight. Less than a year later, though, we landed on the moon! Seven years to plan, nine months to execute. Was that really time wasted?

Judge for yourself. Take some time to write down relationship goals for each major client you currently have. Do you want more revenue from them? More referrals? Where does your relationship fall on the Depth of Relationship Model? Why isn't it deeper?

Now put yourself in their shoes. What are their goals, their needs, their hopes, their fears? What have you done for them — more importantly, perhaps, what have you done for them *lately*?

Lay out a course of action to build that relationship. Jot down ideas for sustaining contact, delivering value and going above and beyond their expectations. Think about ways to thank them as well as ways to help them both professionally and personally.

Be specific. Be detailed. Be bold.

Practice Hard

A good plan is the necessary first step. But, just like basketball, knowing the Xs and Os of the gamebook doesn't mean you can flawlessly execute the offense the first time you step on the court. We learn by doing, and there's no substitute for experience.

Can you practice relationship building? Absolutely. It's a skill like any other. There may be folks for whom it comes more easily (Relaters, I'm thinking about you here), but everyone benefits from practice. Greatness, whether in sports or in business, is dependent more on persistence than on natural talent.

Practice finding new ways to connect people in your network. Practice making the time to regularly call your best clients. Practice setting aside time to plan and visualize success. Practice how you approach prospects and how you pitch your product or service offerings, focusing on what benefits the customer. And yes, even practice planning!

Routine is key to effective practice, as any athlete can tell you. So practice setting routines. I used to hate early mornings, but trained myself to get up and productively use those few hours before the crush of the business day closes in. I spent the time preparing for my day, studying business and self-help books, learning everything about the products and services we offered.

> "When you rise in the morning, form a resolution to make the day a happy one for a fellow creature."
>
> — Sydney Smith

Now I love my early morning time. I've found that by the time the business day "starts," my energy level and enthusiasm are higher, and I feel more productive. Uninterrupted by phone calls or e-mails, I now use that time to scan websites, magazines and newspapers for information that might benefit one of my clients. I think about how to create synergy between people in my network and how to deliver value and create positive ripples for the people I know — and the ones I want to know better.

Execute Thoroughly

If you've done your planning and practicing, the execution should be easy. The Apollo astronauts consistently remarked that after thousands of hours in the simulator practicing lunar landings, the real thing was almost anticlimactic. For all intents and purposes, it felt as though they'd done it hundreds of times before. The key, they said, was sticking to the checklist, taking it one step at a time and not allowing themselves to become distracted. Good advice.

Distraction kills or wounds a lot of fundamentally sound relationship-building plans. We plan to call a client just to check in . . . and then get distracted by a project that takes longer than anticipated. We plan to send out a thank-you note after a meeting . . . and then get distracted by a flurry of phone calls. We plan to send out a regular newsletter to keep our clients informed . . . and somehow never do because we're distracted by meetings, deadlines, crises and new sales opportunities.

If you believe that building relationships is key to your business success, then it's vital that you not allow yourself to become distracted. I know that's easier said than done — life has a way of throwing us curve balls when we expect sliders. But you cannot lose focus.

It's often helpful to make your business relationship building a team activity. Doing so not only helps spread out the work, it enforces accountability. Treat it like you would any other marketing initiative or client account. Set deadlines and stick to 'em. Don't lose out on the tremendous benefits of building relationships simply because you "never got around to it" or "ran out of time."

As you build relationships with customers, vendors and employees, keep a few guidelines in mind:

- *Be sincere.* It doesn't take people long to sense insincerity or ulterior motives, and once they do that relationship is probably fatally wounded. Don't just sound sincere. Be sincere.

- *Be respectful.* Don't waste people's time or impose upon them unnecessarily. The Golden Rule is still the gold standard here, as far as I'm concerned. Treat others the way you would want them to treat you.

- *Be consistent.* Rome wasn't built in a day, and neither are lasting relationships. One lunch won't turn someone into a client for life, and one newsletter won't bring Michael Dell knocking on your door. It takes time, so be patient. Just keep delivering the same exceptional value, keep sending the same others-focused message and keep generating the same positive ripples. I can't emphasize strongly enough the necessity to follow up all relationship-building opportunities in a timely, consistent way.

- *Be a resource.* Look for new and innovative ways to deliver value to your stakeholders. Remember that whiz kid in school everyone wanted to have as a study partner? Strive to play that role for your clients. Create a relationship in which they're willing — even eager — to ask your opinion and solicit your advice. Give freely, without strings, and make every contact with them a memorable and valuable event.

Review Dispassionately

Experience is the best teacher. Unfortunately, it's also a hard teacher. And it's easy to become discouraged when the time, energy and resources we've invested in our relationship-building activities fail to bear fruit. The temptation, all too often, is to simply give up.

That's an understandable reaction, but it's the wrong one. We have to train ourselves in those situations to look at what happened with our heads, not just our hearts. We may be disappointed, frustrated, hurt, even angry — but if we can force ourselves to just get past that, there's tremendous potential to learn, grow and even profit from the experience.

Experience is the best teacher. Unfortunately, it's also a hard teacher.

Again, the Apollo program offers a good example. The astronaut crew of Apollo 1 perished in a fire during a routine test on the launchpad. In the tragedy's aftermath, a number of powerful politicians called for the program's cancellation. But cooler heads prevailed, and after an exhaustive investigation, NASA corrected a number of faulty procedures that, if left unchecked, would almost certainly have caused more deaths in the future. As a result of the fire, the entire organization also rallied around the mission and re-dedicated itself to safety.

When I lose deals (and yeah, I'm sure I lose as many as anyone in sales), I always send a letter thanking the prospect for their time and consideration. I explain that I look at every experience as a learning opportunity and ask permission to contact them within the next few days to discuss the particulars of why they didn't choose to go forward with the transaction. I let them know that this isn't some attempt to change their mind, but rather a genuine request to discover information that will help me better serve future prospects and customers.

Before making the call, I review (on paper) the whole history of my interaction with the prospect, from first contact to that final letter. Taking a deep breath, I conduct an extensive personal inventory of my handling of the account. I look for areas where I feel I might have been under-prepared or off my game. This exercise in introspection isn't always easy, but it *is* always beneficial, particularly in creating talking points for the upcoming phone conversation. Was the prospect put off by a lack of references? By your emphasis on features instead of benefits? By your failure to address one of their fundamental company needs? Look at the entire process from the prospect's eyes.

> **"The greatest mistake you can make in life is to be continually fearing that you will make one."**
>
> — *Elbert Hubbard*

Make sure the conversation itself remains positive and on-topic. Ask questions, be polite and thank them for their time. Send a thank-you card immediately and include a few of your business cards. Despite not getting the sale, you've taken some big steps towards building a relationship, and you never know where that might lead. I've had ex-prospects contact me years later to do business, and others who have sent thousands of dollars of referrals my way. Just goes to show that you never really know where a ripple you create may lead!

Your personal review should help you address any weaknesses in your plan, your practice regimen or your execution. It's not an idle exercise. Consciously look for — and promptly act on — the trends you find and the information you uncover. Keep your relationship goals firmly in mind. You *can* achieve them!

Persistence Pays

There's really no magic formula for building successful professional relationships. From my personal experience, every relationship is unique. Trying to use some sort of cookie-cutter approach is guaranteed to fail, perhaps spectacularly. What we've talked about in this chapter are guidelines, not iron-clad rules.

What is important is the spirit in which any relationship building is conducted. There's no substitute for sincerity, no alternative to patience and persistence. You'll have successes and reverses, moments you'll forever cherish and moments you'd like to forget. Building lasting relationships, whether personal or professional, can be messy.

But never forget that it's also tremendously rewarding. Good relationships make for good business — that's just good sense!

Points to Ponder

- The most valuable economic commodity is information.

- Acquiring and disseminating information can help build and strengthen relationships.

- Good businesses consciously nourish key relationships with clients and prospects, vendors and suppliers, and employees and co-workers.

- Strong relationships can often result in better top-of-mind awareness for businesses than misguided high-dollar advertising campaigns.

- To achieve relationship success in business, approach them as you would a championship basketball game: plan wisely, practice hard, execute thoroughly and review dispassionately.

Ripple Exercises

- Identify what types of information might be of benefit to a client or business associate. Set aside 30 minutes to search the internet for relevant items and pass on the best.

- Take time this week to personally thank at least one client, one vendor and one co-worker with a small gift or thank you note. If possible, treat one of them to lunch.

- Using the plan, practice, execute and review framework, evaluate a client account. Identify the most consistently productive aspects of your relationship as well as the areas that need improvement.

In the mid-19th century, the firm of Phelan and Collander was the preeminent American manufacturer of billiard balls. The balls were made of ivory, which made the company dependent on imports from Africa and Asia.

During the 1860s, a severe ivory shortage prompted Phelan and Collander to explore other materials as possible alternatives. The company offered a handsome $10,000 prize to whoever developed a suitable substitute.

John Hyatt, a young printer from Albany, New York, jumped at the chance. After a great deal of experimentation, Hyatt obtained a patent in 1870 for a material made from gun cotton mixed with alcohol and camphor, then heated until pliable, molded into the desired shape and finally allowed to harden.

There is no record of whether Hyatt won the $10,000, but soon the new composite billiard balls were in saloons throughout the country. (The new material did have an interesting side effect: the new balls struck each other with a sound much louder and sharper than the old ivory balls made. It sounded, in fact, remarkably like a gunshot — which no doubt created a number of unexpected ripple effects in rooms filled with armed cowboys.)

Hyatt called the new material celluloid. By 1889, George Eastman was producing celluloid film for still photography. In 1893, using a specially produced strip of Eastman's film, Thomas Edison created what he called his "kinetoscope," which used another Edison invention, the light bulb, and a ratchet system to create the forerunner to modern movies and a multi-billion dollar entertainment industry.

So the next time you're upset about spending $8 on some Hollywood stinker, you know who to blame: John Hyatt.

7 | RIPPLES IN MOTION
Real-life stories of the ripple effect

It's hard to assess the impact of the ripple effect in pure mathematical terms. But it's easy to see the positive changes in the lives of those affected by the ripples themselves: success, fulfillment, inspiration, friendship, love. Ripple results are often dramatic, fantastic . . . and unexpected.

I've been an avid collector of ripple stories for several years. I love hearing about how chance encounters lead to lifelong friendships, about how opportunities are created and dreams achieved. I love to see destinies being created and fates changed.

Below are a favorite few ripple stories. I hope you enjoy them, are inspired by them and learn something from them. I know I have.

The Christmas Present

Austin banker, businessman and civic leader Jeff Nash knows a thing or two about ripples and relationships. In addition to his position as president of Treaty Oak Bank, Jeff has served on the boards of a number of local organizations, including the Austin Lyric Opera, Ballet Austin and the American Heart Association.

He served as campaign co-chair for the United Way in 2001 and as vice-chair for the Greater Austin Chamber of Commerce, which named him 2000's "Outstanding Board Member." Jeff is also a Trustee for the SafePlace Foundation and has served 18 years on the Board and Executive Committee for the Star of Texas

Fair and Rodeo, including a stint as Board president in 1994. And that's not all — he's also a member of the Executive Council for the Texas Exes Alumni Association at the University of Texas.

Jeff's service-oriented philosophy is rooted in childhood lessons he learned watching his father manage the service department of a large truck dealership. Despite the pressures of managing this business, Jeff's dad consistently and consciously put people first. He not only taught his young son the importance of doing the right thing; he showed him.

Austin banker and civic leader Jeff Nash's service-oriented philosophy is rooted in childhood lessons he learned from his father.

One memory in particular stands out for Jeff. Leaving one Christmas Eve to celebrate the holiday with out-of-town family, Jeff's dad wanted to make a final stop at the shop, probably to pick up some present he had hidden earlier. Almost in front of the building, the Nashes found a car that had broken down on the side of the road. The young couple that owned it had been traveling out of state to visit their own family when the old car simply gave out.

Without hesitation, Jeff's dad took charge of the situation, helping the stranded husband push the car into one of the shop's repair bays. On his own time and at his own expense, he repaired the couple's car. He wasn't concerned about whether or not they could afford it. He didn't complain about the delay to his own holiday plans. He simply rolled up his sleeves and went to work and, in doing so, saved Christmas for another young family.

Jeff never forgot that lesson. More than a lesson, it was a father's gift — a Christmas gift that made a tremendous impact and, through that impact, created innumerable positive ripples. Today, Jeff uses that people-first approach in both business and community service, and the result has been profound and far-reaching. He has raised money for heart disease research, established scholarships for deserving young people, assisted companies in raising capital, created safe havens for victims of domestic abuse, and helped hundreds of Austinites move closer to achieving their own dreams of success and happiness.

Fight for Sight

One of my all-time heroes is my father, whose courage and determination in the face of adversity have created a multitude of ripples. Several years ago, he was diagnosed with macular degeneration, a debilitating eye disease. It progressed rapidly, forcing him to retire early and stop driving. Eventually, he was declared legally blind.

Many people — perhaps even most people — would have withdrawn from the world into a cocoon of personal misery. Not Dad. Although his disease was immensely frustrating to him, he used it to create a number of positive ripples.

Once Dad could no longer drive, one of the first things he did was to re-acquaint himself with the local Albuquerque bus system. My sisters and I weren't thrilled to have our nearly-blind father riding alone on a transit system that was often dangerous, but dad was adamant. And, despite our concerns, we obviously didn't want him confined to his house.

We needn't have worried. Dad was soon riding all over the city and befriending all sorts of fellow travelers. Even the toughest-looking hombres were no match for his engaging manner. He developed friendships with people throughout Albuquerque, including some of the mentally challenged who depended on the bus system. His personality, experience and example made a big impact on many of those he encountered.

Dad also became very active in the Veterans Administration's Commission for the Blind, participating in many of the terrific training programs the Commission offered. He created such positive ripples that the Governor of New Mexico appointed him to the State Commission for the Blind, where he helped create and influence legislation affecting the visually challenged, and particularly senior citizens who were blind or visually challenged. In that role alone, he created ripples whose effects will last for a long, long time.

Despite all the obstacles he faced, Dad never complained,

never lapsed into self-pity, never allowed himself to become a prisoner of his disease. He was forced to make some significant life changes, but he was still *his* life. He refused to surrender his dignity, his optimism or his faith in a loving God. And he took matters into his own hands, learning about alternative methods of combating his disease and educating others in turn. He became a regular speaker at senior centers and a contributor to several area newspapers.

My father stands as proof that no matter what life sends your way, with the right attitude you can transform negative experiences into positive ripples.

His never-give-in, never-say-die attitude led him to try a whole series of homeopathic treatments. He began eating certain vegetables for their specific eye health benefits. He walked every day to exercise his body. Those actions created some really unexpected ripples — his vision actually began to gradually and markedly improve!

Perhaps the most dramatic ripple effect was when his vision improved to the point he could reclaim his driver's license, one of the proudest days of his life. Today he continues to drive, focus on his health (and encourage others diagnosed with macular degeneration) and care for my mother, who suffers from Alzheimer's disease.

My father stands as proof that no matter what life sends your way, with the right attitude you can transform negative experiences into positive ripples. Through what I call his "second life's journey," he has touched, inspired, encouraged, educated, comforted and impacted countless lives. What a legacy!

A Friend in Need

My sister Sheri is another example of courage in the face of poor health. She shares this story about her fight with cancer and the positive ripples even a negative experience can generate:

"The power of human connections is never more powerful than in time of great need. The human spirit is far greater than we expect as we fly through our busy days, ignoring time to take care of ourselves, let alone relationships with family and friends. 9/11 was an incredible example of the human spirit in time of need. Closer to home for me has been an eight-year-battle with an incurable form of Non-Hodgkins Lymphoma, most recently culminating in a bone marrow transplant.

"Within six months of our relocation to Denver, I started down a path of the harshest chemotherapy I'd ever experienced in preparation for the transplant. It would leave me dependent on others for months. There was a profound sense of emptiness, as I knew I had left my network of 11 years, including my dearest friends and business associates, that I had always counted on for emotional support. On my new job only two months, I hadn't yet built much of a network with my new associates and hadn't found a whole lot in common yet with the neighbors. As a wife and mother, I felt helpless without a support system in place to help our family through this time.

> **"The human spiritual connection is far beyond what we see."**

"Of course my family was tremendous, each willing to do anything needed to help save my life. To my surprise, however, not only did I find a huge amount of support from my friends at a distance, but also an amazing amount of support from people I hadn't even met in Colorado, both in the neighborhood, church and my new place of employment. Networks formed without my even trying. Brief encounters with neighbors spiraled out to their friends; meals came from people I didn't even know. Cards, well-wishes and prayers came from family and friends all over the country; I was literally on prayer lists across the nation.

"The human spiritual connection is far beyond what we see. I can't tell you how many angels came my way throughout this treatment. A phone call, a card, an e-mail, a visit or an inspirational word or gift given at just the right time from family and friends always seemed to get me past the next hurdle. The biggest angel of all was my younger sister, who was willing to make the sacrifice that would save my life: a bone marrow transplant.

"I thank God every day for the energy, spirit and prayers

from people everywhere that have been a huge part of my success."

A Call in the Night

The phone rang at shortly after midnight, and Chris knew
it couldn't be good news. It was his friend Tim, and he sounded
distraught and desperate. Almost in tears, he told Chris that he
and his girlfriend had had a huge fight, and she had left him. A
recovering alcoholic, Tim said he was now calling from his cell
phone with six shots of whiskey sitting in front of him. The only
thing that made him hesitate to lift that first shot glass to his lips
was the strength of his relationship with Chris.

That relationship, which had developed in the space of just
a few short months, was something completely unexpected. The
two men met at an Alcoholics Anonymous meeting and instantly
connected. Chris had been sober for nearly five years and knew
the struggles Tim would face during his first months of clean
living. The two men struck up a casual friendship, shooting the
breeze over coffee during a meeting break or grabbing a burger
afterward. And then Tim unexpectedly asked Chris to be his AA
sponsor — a decision that sent their relationship down a very different path.

Hearing Chris talk about the responsibility that comes with
being a sponsor is an eye-opening experience. It shows the power,
trust and vulnerability of the personal relationship like few other examples. And it isn't really about friendship. It's something
deeper, something closer to the bond we talked about in the Depth
of Relationship Model.

Often, like in Tim's case, the sponsor is the person a recovering alcoholic calls just before taking a drink. Often it's that
sponsor's influence that gives them the strength to resist the temptation. And often the sponsor is the only one who can talk them
off that ledge and into a meeting before it's too late. Talk about
the power of relationships!

Chris and Tim's relationship was no different. Because it
was centered around trust and mutual understanding, Tim was

able to confide in Chris like he could with no one else. And Chris, in turn, was able to cut to the heart of the situation and say things to Tim no one could. (Chris once told me that his relationship with Tim was second only to his relationship with his wife, Tracey.)

Thanks to the strength of that relationship, Chris was able to help Tim deal with his crisis without taking a drink that night. It was a victory in a very personal war, and more battles are undoubtedly ahead for both men. But the relationship they've forged with each other has given them an unflinching ally. Being responsible for each other helps keep each of them focused on creating positive ripples for each other and for themselves.

A Teacher's Influence

Jay Stephenson was my high school marketing education teacher and DECA coordinator. He was also one of the first people to truly get me excited about the prospect of becoming an entrepreneur one day. Most importantly, though, he was really one of the first people to teach me the importance of building the kind of strong interpersonal relationships that would significantly increase my chances of success in business . . . and life.

> **"Example is the school of mankind, and they will learn at no other."**
>
> — Edmund Burke

As the school's DECA coordinator, it was Mr. Stephenson's job to educate juniors and seniors about the ways of the world of business. He not only taught his students the "why's" and "how's" of commerce, he also taught them about the American Dream. His obvious excitement helped him connect with kids who ordinarily could not have cared less about school, much less business. Although everyone in his classes knew he was the boss (in a sense, we were his employees), he had a knack for breaking down walls and making us all feel like his equals. He made us all want to learn.

I doubt Mr. Stephenson ever thought his ripple effect would have such a profound impact on so many lives, but it has. He is without a doubt one of the main reasons I am where I am today. I consider myself fortunate to have been one of his students, and even more fortunate to have developed a friendship with him as an adult.

His example should be a beacon to all educators. Forget all the standardized tests and new technologies — at the heart of any successful school system is the relationship between teacher and student and the amazing opportunity that results to positively impact a young person's mental and emotional development. I wish all my teacher friends could see it in that light, just like Mr. Stephenson did. Finding ways to connect with their students is both a responsibility and a privilege, and perhaps the most important ripple they can create. Mr. Stephenson didn't have any tricks or slick techniques; he was about to connect with even the most distant kids primarily due to one thing: effort!

He put forth the effort to get to know each and every one of his kids as if they were his own. His sincere, determined focus broke down barriers and helped him find the best strategy for facilitating the learning process. How good was he? Within a few weeks, he could transform even the roughest, toughest kids in class into thoughtful, respectful and well-mannered young people. He shot straight with his students, telling them what he expected and showing them how to accomplish it. He made it a priority to build a relationship with each child and, not surprisingly, when he did the child excelled.

Whether you are a teacher, parent, uncle or aunt, distant cousin or simply an authority figure in a child's life, consider what tremendous ripples might result from a sincere effort to connect with him or her. Think about the effects on them, their families, their future — even on our society as a whole.

Music Man

Jim had been visiting the same coffee shop almost every morning for a year and a half. Randy, one of the shop's employees, had served Jim his cup of java almost every morning for a year and half. But despite the frequency of their contact, in all that time, the two men had exchanged only passing comments about the weather.

That changed on September 12, 2001, the morning after the most devastating terrorist attack the U.S. had ever known. Jim walked into the shop, still red-eyed and dazed from watching nonstop news coverage of the attack's aftermath. Although he went through the motions, both the day and the shop seemed somehow different, even surreal.

Jim ordered his usual latte, and Randy silently began preparing it. Unexpectedly, he dropped the filter. On impulse, Jim asked him if he was OK. To both of their surprise, Randy started to tear up.

"I'm just so angry and shocked," he said. "I never thought it would affect me like this, but this is the last place I want to be today."

"I know what you mean," said Jim. "I almost called in sick myself this morning. But I started thinking that, in some little way, staying home was like admitting defeat. The terrorists would win. And I couldn't do that, so I dragged myself out of bed after all."

With that, a long-delayed relationship was born. Over the next few months, the two became fast friends. Randy even learned of Jim's growing interest in jazz and invited him to stop by the coffee house one evening to hear his jazz band play. Jim eagerly took him up on it, showing up the very next night, something that clearly made an impact on Randy.

Randy's passion and musical talent immediately impressed Jim, who saw a mild-mannered coffee shop employee transformed into an engaging and accomplished performer. For his part, Randy was floored that his new friend had actually taken the time to come, especially when so many longtime friends kept promising and never showing. Jim's simple gift of his time made a big impression and helped cement their friendship.

A fairly well-connected businessman, Jim had met several people with ties to the local music scene. He decided to call in some favors to help give Randy's band the chance it deserved. A few phone calls later and Randy was being asked to audition at some of the city's trendiest music venues.

Before long, the band was in high demand, and their weekend gigs had turned into nightly events. The nocturnal schedule and new source of income prompted Randy to leave the coffee shop to focus on his musical career full-time — something he'd wanted to do for years. Thanks to a chance conversation with a customer who became a friend, he was now able to live his dream.

Work Out Warriors

Mike had always felt very insecure about going to the gym. Overweight and self-conscious of his appearance, he wanted to work out but dreaded the meat market atmosphere that pervaded the gym in the evenings. He was painfully aware of the amused looks and barely concealed smirks of the "beautiful people" as he struggled with one machine or another. Not surprisingly, his insecurity only increased.

Mike eventually shifted his work schedule to allow him to exercise during the afternoon, when the gym was practically empty. He immediately felt more comfortable and started looking forward again to his regular work out sessions. Until one day, that is . . .

"No one can make you feel inferior without your consent."

— Eleanor Roosevelt

While working out on one of the gym's stationary bikes, Mike saw a good-looking, heavily-muscled man walk over and ask if the bike next to his was taken. Mike smiled and shook his head no, while inside he silently raged. "No," he thought. "This is the wrong time for you to be here. If you people start coming now, I'll never be able to work out!"

For a few minutes, the two men peddled in silence. Then the new Adonis asked Mike his name, something none of the other "beautiful people" had ever done. Startled, Mike blurted it out while staring straight ahead.

"My name's Rob," said Mr. Muscle. Mike said nothing.

A few minutes passed, and Rob said, "Isn't this great? We have the gym all to ourselves!" Great, thought Mike, that's just what we needed: more of you people moving in on *our* time.

Rob, still not taking the hint, asked, "So do you work out here everyday?"

"I do. Why do you ask?"

"No reason, " Rob said. "I just used to come here during the day and hadn't seen you before." Mike looked over at him and mentally acknowledged the possibility that maybe Mr. Muscle was just trying to be friendly. "I was overweight and hated coming during the meat market times — and still do. I usually get up early and come in before work, but starting today my work schedule is changing so I guess I'll be switching back to afternoon work outs."

Mike smiled and nodded, silently surprised that this guy could have ever been overweight. They chatted off and on for the next few minutes and learned that they had some similar interests. During subsequent work out sessions, they traded small talk and friendly waves across the gym.

It was clear, though, that Mike was still holding back, and that he felt absolutely inadequate next to his new friend. Finally Rob confronted the issue. "Mike, I get the feeling sometimes that you're a little uncomfortable around me," he said. "The thing you'll find about me is that I'm brutally honest and direct. My wife calls it a personality flaw, but it's served me well for a long time. So what's bothering you?"

Just like that, the floodgates opened and Mike shared his insecurities and fear of being mocked. Rob listened in silence until Mike had finished. Then he told him that he understood, having struggled in the past with his own weight problem. But, he reassured Mike, he wasn't about to judge him on what he looked like or how much he could bench. He liked Mike for who he was, not for who other people expected him to be.

Mike instantly felt a surge of relief and acceptance. The two men continued to discuss the difficulties of losing weight, and Rob told Mike how hard it was for him doing it without a friend pushing him, encouraging him and holding him accountable. He volunteered to be there for Mike, acting as a guide, coach, mentor and cheerleader — or whatever else Mike needed. With that generous offer, the emotional foundation for a deep and long-lasting friendship was laid.

Mike had gone to the gym looking for a better waistline and ended up with a friend. Despite their different appearances, Rob and Mike weren't all that different from each other. And Mike also learned how easily he might've missed out on an important relationship by pre-judging someone according to the same criteria he himself resented being judged by. He learned two of life's most important lessons: don't judge a book by its cover . . . and you never know where a ripple will end up.

On and On and On . . .

There are as many stories about the ripple effect as there are ripples themselves. What are the most significant stories in your life? What relationships, perhaps formed by chance, have most impacted you? How would your career, your friendships, your family be different if someone else hadn't created a ripple in the great pond of life?

I want to hear about your ripple stories! Log on to our website, **www.therippleeffectbook.com**, and share your favorites.

Points to Ponder

- Everyone has a story showing how the ripple effect has impacted their life and the lives of those around them.

- Ripple stories span gender, generation, ethnicity and geography.

- Even relatively small actions can result in far-reaching and powerful ripples.

Ripple Exercises

- Identify a story from your own experience that demonstrates the reach and power of the ripple effect. Take the time to write it down.

- Gather another ripple story from a friend, family member or business associate.

In the 18th century, paper was still being made from cloth. The process, largely unchanged from ancient Chinese methods, was slow and tedious. Even a good papermaker could turn out only about 750 sheets a day.

Cloth had another drawback — there simply wasn't enough of it to keep up with the skyrocketing demand for paper products. Sometime in the early 18th century, a French scientist named René-Antoine Ferchault de Réaumur — chemist, physicist, mathematician and amateur entomologist — noticed during a walk in the woods an abandoned wasp's nest. Looking more closely, he realized that the nest was made from paper.

Obviously, the wasps weren't making the paper from cloth. Réaumur theorized that they must be using wood, processing it in their stomachs to create a crude but durable paper. If they could do it chemically, Réaumur speculated, perhaps the process could be replicated. Although he never produced even a single sheet of paper from wood, his writings inspired others to try their hand.

One was Jacob Christian Schäffer, a German clergyman, who between 1765 and 1771 tried making paper from 80 different vegetables, including cabbage and potatoes. His success was spotty, but he published his writings in six volumes.

It did pave the way for Mattias Koops, a Dutchman living in London in 1850. He set up the first paper mill that processed a combination of wood and straw to make paper — and went bankrupt when a conservative British public refused to buy the new-fangled paper.

About the same time, though, Friedrich Gottlieb Keller, a German weaver inspired by Réaumur's original work, invented a machine that pulped wood with a spinning grinding stone. Another German, Heinrich Voelter, bought Keller's patent and built improved production versions of the machine. In 1868, the first wood-pulp newspaper in the U.S. was published; by the 1880s, wood-pulp paper was being more widely used than rag-paper.

Today, over 90% of our paper is made from wood, the result of ripples that began with a stroll in the woods 250 years ago.

8 | NO TIME TO WASTE

Making the most of your opportunities

At the beginning of this book, we talked about the need to take stock of your life and ask yourself some tough questions: When my time is up, what legacy will I leave behind? How will I have impacted the people in my life? Did I use my time here as wisely and well as I could have?

I was reminded again of that on a recent Monday morning when I received a call telling me that Marvin, a longtime friend and client, had passed away. "You were one of the people he wanted to make sure was notified," his assistant told me. "He always loved working with you."

Marvin and I had been unlikely friends for more than a dozen years. A gruff, tough, no-nonsense old executive, he regularly terrified salespeople and vendors who darkened his door. But I soon discovered that his bark was much worse than his bite, and that beneath that hardened shell was a gracious, helpful person with a tremendous store of life experience and business knowledge.

Gradually, Marvin came to trust me, eventually buying almost all his office equipment from me over the years and relying on me for input on other technology issues with which he was unfamiliar. I was even able to help him in other facets of his business, connecting him with my corporate insurance broker when he wanted to lower his premiums. As with many of my other recommendations, he listened carefully, followed up immediately and came away very pleased with the results.

During the course of our relationship, Marvin and I met

probably 40+ times. Our meetings usually ran long, primarily because he loved to recount detailed stories of his past business challenges, successes and mistakes. He wasn't just telling them to hear himself talk, though. Every story had a lesson, a clear message he wanted me to hear and internalize. I came to cherish each visit with Marvin, collecting his stories like the pearls of wisdom they were.

When I told Marvin last year that I was starting a new business, he took the news that I wouldn't be directly supporting his office supply needs hard. Then, in his typical fashion, he began comparing this change to the many challenges and opportunities he'd encountered during his long career, drawing out the handful of life lessons he wanted me to learn. He told me that he was confident I would be successful in anything I took on.

As I was leaving, Marvin turned to me and said, "Steve, I've known you for a long time, and you've always been one of my favorite people to visit with and to do business with." He shook my hand, looked me squarely in the eye and smiled that sly, mischievous smile of his. "I'm proud of you, Steve. Thank you."

That was the last time I saw Marvin.

At his memorial service, I was struck by the number of people he had touched through his life and business. His presence was almost palpable, like a warm blanket covering and comforting us. Marvin wasn't the easiest man to get to know. But for those of us who were fortunate enough to do so, the rewards were great. He and I connected like few others in my career, and the lessons I learned from him over years have proven invaluable. I know he'd love that I'm sharing my passion for people and the power of relationships. For me, Marvin was always a tremendous supporter, as well as a loyal customer, a wonderful business influence, a knowledgeable advisor, a concerned mentor and, most importantly, a good friend.

Surround Yourself with Excellence

In the preceding chapters, we've talked a great deal about different personality types and different types of relationships.

We've seen that people interact differently, and that while there are some universal guidelines to building relationships, each relationship itself is as unique as any snowflake.

Hopefully, you've seen in these pages some of the awesome power of the ripple effect, how even seemingly minor actions can reverberate through our network of relationships and create dramatic results. Everyone on this planet is interconnected at some degree. All we have to do is be willing to tap into the energy of those connections.

For me, the ripple effect is more than a theory. It's a way of life. It's changed how I run my businesses, how I treat people, how I measure success, how I see the world . . . and how I see myself. It's become the genie of my own personal Aladdin's cave, opening new doors, new opportunities and new adventures.

> **For me, the ripple effect is more than a theory. It's a way of life. It's changed how I run my businesses, how I treat people, how I measure success, how I see the world . . . and how I see myself.**

With this book, I've laid out a basic relationship road map for you to follow. But the map is simply the beginning; it's the journey itself that matters. Where you go, who'll you meet and what you'll find at the end of your journey — that's for you to find out. I hope you're as eager to get started as I am.

Your choice of traveling companions is important. Being true to a relationship-centered lifestyle takes time, patience and effort. You'll need support along the way, people to encourage and sustain you. Those relationships in particular will have a powerful and lasting impact on your life. Choose wisely.

Surround yourself with people who display the same virtues you want for yourself, both professionally and personally. Let those people guide you and teach you. Absorb the positive energy and confidence they exude, and internalize those attributes and characteristics.

The flip side of that, of course, is to steer clear of folks with negative "people karma." You know who I mean — people who expect the worst and usually find it, in both other people and in situations. And their negativity is infectious, polluting (and sometimes even destroying) friendships, families and companies. Their behavior is both self-defeating and, unfortunately, self-perpetuating. Get too close to these people and you're likely to be sucked into the vortex they almost instinctively generate.

All of us are given only a finite time on this earth. Make the most of yours. Seek out those relationships that will benefit you and those around you, relationships that will help you achieve your potential and become a better, more enlightened person. Don't waste your time in relationships that sap your energy, strength and vision.

Obviously, though, you can't go through life entirely steering clear of unpleasant people. Let's face it, sooner or later you're going to have to deal with negative people, maybe a lot of them, in probably every facet of your life. How do you avoid being drawn into their negativity?

For me, the solution is actually pretty simple. First, I make a conscious decision not to be influenced by their negativity. Just being on your guard can be a very effective defense. Second, for every minute I have to spend with a negative person, I spend five minutes with positive, upbeat people. Doing so re-energizes and reinvigorates me, and makes those negative encounters seem much less significant.

Having said all that, I have to confess that I haven't pruned negative people out of my life completely. I have several friends who tend toward the dark side, and I've taken it upon myself to be a positive force in their lives. I hope that some of my attitude and philosophy will rub off on them, gradually bringing them around to a happier, more productive way of living. I try to do the same with other negative people I may casually encounter — sometimes with rewarding results.

One thing is sure, though. I refuse to allow their negativity to warp my perspective. Life's just too short.

Connecting with Your Past

While the ripples we create can extend into time and space,

influencing people still unborn, I think an important component of living a relationship-centered life is to connect with your own past. As Winston Churchill once said, "The further you can look behind, the further you can look ahead."

It recently struck me that I know relatively little about my family history. Sure, I heard stories growing up, but I frankly did my best to tune them out. They seemed boring and occasionally embarrassing, and they certainly didn't seem to have any importance for *my* life.

The older I get, the more I regret that youthful ignorance. I want to know more about where I came from, the people who shaped me and the people who shaped them. Perhaps more importantly, I've been able to appreciate my parents as unique individuals, not just as *my parents*.

That shift in my viewpoint really started as I watched my dad deal with his macular degeneration (see Chapter Seven for the whole story). His courage, optimism, persistence and faith in the face of what seemed like unbeatable odds reaffirmed him as one of the heroes in my life. I wanted to know more about him: his childhood, his dreams, his fears, his proudest moments, his greatest regrets. I'd already absorbed many of the values he not only preached, but practiced. I'd learned from him the importance of, in whatever you're doing, focusing on the task at hand and buckling down until it's done. I'd learned tenacity and the value of hard work.

But there was still a lot I didn't know, a lot of questions I wanted answered. For my mother, now in the late stages of Alzheimer's disease, it's already too late to ask those questions and hear those invaluable perspectives on life and family. I didn't want to have the same regrets with my father.

So I've begun, consciously and intentionally, trying to connect with him as a person. I've started asking him all sorts of questions: What made you fall in love with Mom? Why did you decide on a career in engineering rather than art (he is a gifted artist and woodworker)? Were there any goals you had that you didn't achieve? What success are you proudest of? My ad-hoc interviews have led to some terrific discussions, some fascinating insights and some invaluable information I'll one day pass onto my sons. And with any luck, Dad and I will have many more years for these kinds of conversations — but I'm not taking anything for granted.

This ongoing dialogue has also strengthened the relationship my father and I have. It's helped us connect on a level we hadn't previously reached. And I know he's been flattered that I want to know what makes him tick and hear all about his life story. Just talking about certain memories can warm the heart and brighten the day.

My challenge to you is to do the same with a parent or grandparent, or even with a sibling or old friend. Set aside some time for creative questioning and deep, sincere conversation. Just by making the effort, I think your relationship will move to a new level. Who knows what ripples will result?

Karma = Action

Ripples are the result of action. Relationships are the result of effort. Unless you're willing to accept that, you won't create positive ripples or build productive relationships. It's not enough to read about it or think about it or dream of the possibilities. If you want to see the power of the ripple effect, you've got to act!

I mentioned a little earlier what I call "people karma," the phenomenon of people generally getting what they expect. Positive people seem to find opportunity and success with far greater frequency than negative people. Why? I believe in part it's because they are creating more powerful ripples. They act with the expectation of success, and more often than not they are rewarded.

I used to think that karma was a pretty passive notion; you were pretty much on the receiving end of whatever fate had in store for you. But that's mistaken, says no less an authority than the Dalai Lama. "One will understand that karma means 'action.' Karma is a very active process," he writes in *The Art of Happiness.* "And when we talk of karma, or action, it is the very action committed by an agent, in this case, ourselves, in the past. So what kind of future will come about, to a large extent, lies within our own hands at present. It will be determined by what initiatives we take now."

Isn't that really just another way of describing the ripple effect? The kind of future you create for yourself begins today. You plant its seeds in the lives you touch, the relationships you nurture, the help you unstintingly give others.

Don't wait — make the changes today! Create ripples in the lives of those around you: family, friends, coworkers, employees, vendors, casual acquaintances, clients and neighbors. Start now, start small and think big!

I'll close with another quote from the Dalai Lama:

"If you maintain a feeling of compassionate, loving kindness, then something automatically opens your inner door. Through that, you can communicate much more easily with other people. And that feeling of warm creates a kind of openness. You'll find that all human beings are just like you, so you'll be able to relate to them more easily.

"But there is another source of worth and dignity from which you can relate to other fellow human beings. You can relate to them because you are still a human being, within the human community. You share that bond. And that human bond is enough to give rise to a sense of worth and dignity."

Good luck, Godspeed and happy rippling.

Points to Ponder

- To make success a habit, surround yourself with examples of success, integrity and generosity. Avoid overly negative or critical people, or at least take steps to ensure that their defeatist attitudes don't infect you.

- Take the time to discover (or rediscover) your own story by connecting with family members and strengthening those relationships.

- Ripples are the result of action and intention. What ripples can you create right now?

Ripple Exercises

- Set aside time to interview an older family member about their childhood, career and formative life events. Record the interview.

- Identify three people you admire as role models. Use the Connector Model in Chapter Three to find someone in your network who can connect you and enlist their help.

RECOMMENDED READING

Blink
By Malcolm Gladwell
Little, Brown

Leading the Revolution
By Gary Hamel
Plum

The Human Fabric
By Bijoy Goswami with David
K. Wolpert
Aviri Publishing

Gung Ho!
By Ken Blanchard and Sheldon
Bowles
Morrow

The E-Myth Revisted
By Michael E. Gerber
Harper-Collins

*Swim With the Sharks Without
Being Eaten Alive*
By Harvey Mackay
Ballantine Books

Over the Top
By Zig Ziglar
Thomas Nelson Publishers

The Art of Happiness
By His Holiness The Dalai Lama
and Howard Cutter, M.D.
Riverhead Books

Love is the Killer App
By Tim Sanders
Three Rivers Press

Good to Great
By Jim Collins
Harper Business

*Seven Habits of Highly Effective
People*
By Stephen R. Covey
Simon & Schuster

A Whack on the Side of the Head
By Roger Von Oech
Warner Books

The Anatomy of Buzz
By Emanuel Rosen
Doubleday

The Portable MBS in Strategy
By Liam Fahey and Robert M.
Randall
Wiley

Awaken the Giant Within
By Anthony Robbins
Summit Books

*Never Eat Alone: And Other
Secrets to Success, One Relation-
ship at a Time*
By Keith Ferrazi with Tahl Raz
Currency Books

ABOUT THE AUTHOR

Steve Harper — entrepreneur, consultant, author and speaker — is the founder of SWOT Vision, Inc., a consulting firm that helps companies of all sizes build strong relationships with clients, prospects and employees. He also speaks professionally to a variety of groups, both corporate and civic, about creating positive ripples in their own lives.

Steve lives in Austin, Texas, with his wife, Kathy, and his two sons, Zachary and Joshua. Contact him at steve@swotvision.com.